Three Stars for the Colonel

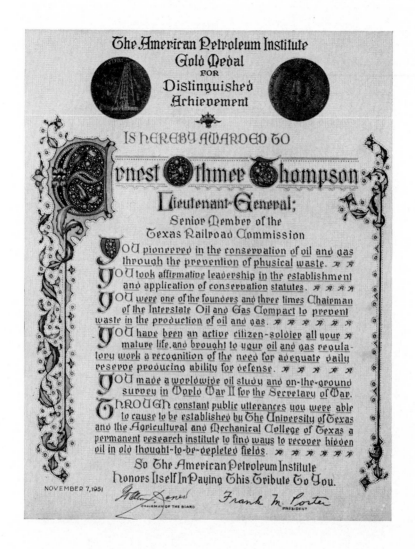

The American Petroleum Institute
Gold Medal
FOR
Distinguished
Achievement

IS HEREBY AWARDED TO

Ernest Othmer Thompson;

Lieutenant-General;

Senior Member of the
Texas Railroad Commission

YOU pioneered in the conservation of oil and gas through the prevention of physical waste.

YOU took affirmative leadership in the establishment and application of conservation statutes.

YOU were one of the founders and three times Chairman of the Interstate Oil and Gas Compact to prevent waste in the production of oil and gas.

YOU have been an active citizen-soldier all your mature life, and brought to your oil and gas regulatory work a recognition of the need for adequate daily reserve producing ability for defense.

YOU made a worldwide oil study and on-the-ground survey in World War II for the Secretary of War.

THROUGH constant public utterances you were able to cause to be established by The University of Texas and the Agricultural and Mechanical College of Texas a permanent research institute to find ways to recover hidden oil in old thought-to-be-depleted fields.

So The American Petroleum Institute
Honors Itself In Paying This Tribute To You.

NOVEMBER 7, 1951

CHAIRMAN OF THE BOARD

Frank M. Porter
PRESIDENT

James A. Clark

Three Stars for the Colonel

Random House   New York

Photo by Edith Miller, reprinted
by special permission of *Business Week*

Copyright, 1954, by James A. Clark

First Printing

All rights reserved under International
and Pan-American Copyright Conventions
Published in New York by Random House, Inc.,
and simultaneously in Toronto, Canada, by
Random House of Canada, Limited

Library of Congress Catalog Card Number: 54-6650

Manufactured in the United States of America

Dedication

Dedicated to the ten independent oil men whose names are listed below because it was they who encouraged and made possible the writing of this book in order to perpetuate the name and deeds of Ernest O. Thompson, who has contributed more than any other man to the petroleum industry and the conservation of oil and gas.

J. S. Abercrombie
R. H. Abercrombie
George R. Brown
Herman Brown
Michel T. Halbouty
Floyd L. Karsten
John W. Mecom
R. E. (Bob) Smith
William A. Smith
Wesley West

Acknowledgments

The author is deeply grateful to the many people whose advice and assistance have made this book possible. To include the entire list of those who have helped would be impractical, but it is desired to give credit at least to the chief sources of information.

James S. Abercrombie, Robert H. Abercrombie, Warren L. Baker, Harry Batis, Brown Booth, Tom Brawner, Marion Brock, George Brown, Herman Brown, E. O. Buck, R. W. Byram, Tom Carnahan, Earl Clark, Olin Culberson, Tom Daily, William N. Finnegan, Elwood Fouts, Charles I. Francis, Michel T. Halbouty, Robert E. Hardwicke, Ken Harper, Governor W. P. Hobby, E. P. Hubbard, Harold Lebourgeois, Tom Lester, Ed Marsten, John W. Mecom, Leroy Menzing, Gene Miller, William J. Murray, Jr., Glenn McCarthy, Val Jean McCoy, Ralph McCullough, J. A. Neath, Don Riddle, Jack Shannon, Charles E. Simons, Emerson Smith, R. E. (Bob) Smith, William A. Smith, John R. Steele, Captain Bill Sterling, John W. Wagner and others contributed substantially to the material in this volume.

Material has been obtained from the files of the following daily newspapers and periodicals: The *Amarillo News-Globe*, the *Houston Post*, the *Amarillo Times*, the *Houston Chronicle*, the *Fort Worth Star-Telegram*, the *Dallas Morning News*, the *Houston Press*, the *Austin American-Statesman*, the *Oklahoma City Daily Oklahoman*, the *El Paso*

Herald-Post, the *Dallas Times-Herald,* the *Tulsa Tribune,* the *Galveston Tribune,* the *Corsicana Sun,* the *San Antonio News-Express,* the *San Antonio Light,* the *Wichita (Falls) Daily Times,* the *Witchita Falls Record-News,* the *Longview News,* the *Tyler Telegraph,* the *Lubbock Avalanche,* the *Kilgore News,* the *Beaumont Enterprise,* the *Beaumont Journal, The Oil and Gas Journal, Business Week, World Oil, Time, The TIPRO Reporter,* and *The Independent.* Also helpful were the records of the Texas Railroad Commission.

Useful to the author in correlating historical and technical information were *Texas Oil and Gas Since 1543* by C. A. Warner; *Flush Production* by Gerald Forbes; *Petroleum Conservation* edited by Stuart E. Buckley; *Oil, Titan of the Southwest* by Carl Coke Rister; *The Handbook of Texas* published by the Texas State Historical Association; *Texas Gas Conservation Laws,* a brief prepared by the Attorney General of Texas (Grover Sellers) and his assistants, James Noel and Elton M. Hyder, Jr. and *Legal History of Oil and Gas, A Symposium* published by the American Bar Association. *Petroleum Facts and Figures,* published by the American Petroleum Institute, was an essential source of statistical information.

John Duncan Kemp, my associate and chief researcher, is entitled to great credit for a remarkable job of collecting facts on the colonel and in collating the Thompson papers as well as contributing his valuable counsel in the writing of *Three Stars for the Colonel.*

A very special acknowledgment goes to Estelle, my wife, who typed the manuscript, and without whose counsel and advice this effort would have been impossible.

JAMES A. CLARK

Contents

Foreword

The history of the production of oil and the substantial dependence of the United States for its economic security upon the stability of the petroleum industry is so filled with the biographies of distinguished and capable men that it has become a legendary part of the epochal story of a great nation.

The measure of all success in any industrial development is primarily gauged by the capabilities of the men who guide the destinies of its activities and is a reflection of their ability, unselfishness and public devotion.

The economy of our great nation in peace and in war is today largely dependent upon the stability and economic progress of petroleum and its allied industries.

We, in this generation, have been even more impressed with the importance of the petroleum industry as a result of having engaged in two great wars, both of which were fought to a large extent by mechanical implementations made possible by the products of crude oil.

Those in the oil business may justly be proud that in this last great conflict every emergency of every hour was met by the petroleum industry.

The magnitude of the industry, its phenomenal

growth, its economic stability and its contribution to national defense result from the courage, determination, foresight, ability and devotion of a few great men who have directed its destinies during the past two decades.

If there is a champion to whom the industry can point as contributing the full measure of intellectual ability, courage, hard work and unselfish leadership, that man is General Ernest O. Thompson.

We could not adequately appraise his full contribution to the welfare of our industry and to the consequent economic stability and progress of our state and nation.

We cannot fully appraise his efforts, his courage, and his determination in difficult times and what they meant to the later security of our nation and to our ultimate victory in the last war, by having preserved a sound and dependable supply of crude petroleum in our hour of great need in one of the most decisive periods of the history of the world.

We remember that during the arduous days of the early 30's the most forthright champion for the conservation of our natural resources and for the orderly development of the petroleum industry was this man who had the courage to back his decisions without faltering and who had the foresight to know that conservation was essential to the maintenance of stability in an industry that was growing like a young giant.

We also remember that when we were divided among ourselves as to the desirability of oil conservation Ernest Thompson was its strongest advocate.

We recall that when there were those in our own industry who could not resist the temptation of quick wealth at whatever cost, Ernest Thompson had the vision to see that such practices could result only in ruin, and the courage to issue and defend the now famous orders of the Texas Railroad Commission that ultimately established the basis for the prevention of physical waste and the conservation of petroleum resources.

These deeds he performed not by being brazen or defiant of people's wishes but by being patient, decisive and intellectual in his judgment.

He was ever willing to utilize the legal and engineering ability with which he was blessed, and was repeatedly willing to submit his efforts to the cold and critical judgment of the law in both State and Federal Courts until a suitable formula for the conservation of our natural resources could be established, agreeable to the sovereignty of the state and to the constitution that protects as sacred the liberties and independence of us all.

It was in these toilsome days when this champion of conservation was criticized, maligned and enjoined that he contributed most to the ultimate protection of petroleum and its products which gave us a supply of plenty in the hazardous days of the war when a failure of that supply might well have meant an end to the democratic way of living on the earth.

How different might have been the fate of our nation, how much lower might be the standard of our economy, if during those days of chaos and trouble there had been at the helm a less able administrator than General Thompson.

Where we might be if he had vacillated in his objectives, if he had yielded to criticism, if he had bowed and submitted to the clamoring voices of dissenting factions within our own industry, we cannot know.

We can only know that where there was chaos he brought forth order; where there was insecurity, he established the basis for stability and where there was waste, he substituted conservation and efficiency.

We can only know that in a large sense Ernest Thompson was the father of the practices and policies in the production and utilization of petroleum and its products that we now know are essential to the stability and the progress of our industry and the security of our nation.

It may be that there will be other achievements in his life that will rank him as a great native son, but for what he has already done in providing a dependable supply of petroleum in peace and for war he has built his own monument of immortality for which a whole people will be forever grateful.

General Thompson has always been a soldier of the front line. In the first great war he left the law school of the University of Texas to become an active American soldier in the defense of free people and emerged from that conflict a distinguished officer. In World War II he was again in the first line of defense after the dark days of Pearl Harbor.

Believing in democracy, he believes in the ultimate sovereignty of the people.

His concept of this nation is a group of united sovereign states with a constitutional division of powers between federal and state government.

He has been quick to sense and eager to champion the

rights of the sovereign states and to defend them against the threat of encroachment of federal regimentation that is not agreeable to the concept of this nation.

He has the confidence that is born of long experience and is ever alert to the furtive efforts of any who would seek by subterfuge to reduce the sovereign power of the states to regulate their own natural resource industries.

When the Anglo-American Oil Agreement was urged upon the American people, he was among the first to oppose its adoption in the full realization that it would make possible the regulation of the domestic oil industry by a treaty commission or by a federal agency empowered to enforce our trade obligations.

Whether it be a proposed international treaty, a national economic policy, a state law or a field regulation, General Thompson has always been on the alert for and quick to detect any move which would take the regulation of our petroleum resources from the hands of the people and put it in those of some faraway bureau commission or federal official. Without being cynical, he is wise to the stratagems that develop behind the scenes and to the various "fronts" which seek to undermine our conservation policies.

He is our champion in every effort at investigation and inquisition and, because of his informed mind and unimpeachable integrity, he is not subject to pressure by those who are unfriendly to our industry and to the sovereign regulation of our state.

The General is not forgetful that governments exist for the benefit of all of the people.

In his efforts as a member of the regulatory body of

Texas, he has been always primarily aware of his responsibility to the citizens of the state whether or not they were engaged in petroleum activities.

He has been a sound and dependable balance wheel in a rapidly growing industry which requires stability for the benefit of the general public, the landowner, the producer, the industrialist, the school children and the public treasury.

He has avoided every effort to contribute to the selfish desires of those who would utilize the powers of his office for purposes of price fixing or private gain and has adhered with unwavering determination to the formula that petroleum is a resource with which we have been endowed by heaven and which we are under obligation to conserve and use wisely for the benefit of all of the people in this generation and in the generations yet to come.

Realizing that stability is essential to the development of the oil industry, he has at the same time been fully aware that the progress of a whole nation, in a mechanical age, is dependent upon an adequate and low-priced supply of fuel and to this end he has untiringly devoted his efforts and ability.

As one of the authors and founders of the Interstate Oil Compact Commission, he has shared with other oil-producing states of the nation the problems that were solved in trying times and has been a primary contributor to the stability of petroleum industries throughout the nation.

As the representative of the President and the Secretary of War, he has investigated the oil resources of the world and is today one of the informed and unimpeachable authorities upon the petroleum problems of two hemispheres.

We pay homage to a great champion of industrial democracy and state sovereignty.

He has been a father of conservation policies in his state and a leader of the conservation efforts of all the oil-producing states in the union. He has been a defender of the state's right to control its own natural resources and has demonstrated the effectiveness of this political philosophy by providing an abundance of oil in peace and war.

He has been a man with great vision, and has so carried out the precepts of his faith as to create an ever-widening market for this indispensable commodity and thereby has been responsible for added income and economic security for thousands.

He has issued without fear or favor official orders dedicated to the preservation of our conservation practices with a keen awareness of the legal, engineering and economic problems involved.

He has given stability and a hopeful future to a great industry and has contributed substantially to the economic soundness of his state.

One has but to look about him to see the monuments General Ernest O. Thompson has erected by his own efforts.

We honor him as a great citizen; we love him as a man of integrity and faith. We trust him as a man of vision and capable leadership.

We extend our grateful thanks for his determination

and valiant fight to protect the economic stability of our people and we consecrate with sincere devotion his accomplishments that have contributed to the welfare of his state and to the preservation and security of his nation.

General Thompson—we salute you!

HONORABLE R. B. ANDERSON
Deputy Secretary of Defense

A speech delivered at
Amarillo, Texas on August 25, 1949.

CHAPTER I

The Black Giant

Beneath the lacework of timbers on a derrick floor a handful of men worked quietly but briskly. The sound of their movements and voices were muffled by the slow grinding of a rotary table and the roar of boiler fires. It was the evening of October 3, 1930 on a Rusk County farm owned by Daisy Bradford in deep East Texas.

A little man in white shirt sleeves, a pork-pie hat and baggy trousers leaned against the derrick leg. He had waited three days for the well to come in and he was tired of waiting. Around him were a scattering of people. The others—tired like the little man—had gone home in disgust convinced that East Texas had one more dry hole.

Those who stayed, like the ones who had left, were mostly poor people, clinging stubbornly to an almost empty hope that this newest try would be different. The depression leaned heavily on East Texas farmers, already burdened with a two-year drought and farmed-out land.

The little man had come out of Oklahoma with a word of optimism. He told East Texas farmers he was going to find oil where the big men said there was no oil. He was a good oil man and a good promoter in spite of his seventy

3

years. The farmers believed him because he knew his business and because they wanted a small hope to lean on. His first two wildcats had failed—but only because of mechanical trouble—and he had not reached his goal. That goal was the oil-bearing stratum known as the Woodbine sand. To drill this third well he had been forced to sell and mortgage much of his holdings to get supplies and to pay his men. His empire of leases had shrunk to the few thousand acres that he still controlled.

This had to be it. If this well failed, he would be broke. Even as he leaned against the derrick leg, the bit was in the Woodbine. It had reached that objective a week before and Ed Laster, the driller, had reported an oil showing and gas odor. The little man would now find out if the experts were right. They said that the great sand section would contain no oil because there was no anticline, no structure where oil could be trapped. The sand pinched out before it reached the Sabine uplift, a massive anticline about one hundred miles across. If the stratum had continued on to fold over the big rise as it approached the river, there might be oil. That's what most of the smart oil men said. There were a few who believed in another theory but they were like Dad Joiner, the little man in the pork-pie hat and the baggy trousers. They were wildcatters, not producers or big company men. Dad Joiner's own geologist, A. D. Lloyd, had a theory that the Woodbine butted up against the Sabine uplift and wedged out to form its own oil trap. A sort of stratigraphic trap, Mr. Lloyd called it. Dad believed with him. So did the poor people of East Texas who had nothing to lose and an oil boom to gain. It's always the

4

men who wander off the charted courses who find the new worlds.

Dad Joiner was leaning against the derrick leg. Ed Laster waved everyone back. Suddenly there was a roar and a long swoosh. Dad snapped out of his thoughts and wheeled around to see oil and gas shooting over the crown block. He felt like shouting, but he was too tired. Anyway he was an undemonstrative little man, shy and almost apologetic. He watched and marveled as the little crowd roared with the rising fluid. He heaved a deep sigh of relief. He didn't dance or shout or grab anyone around the shoulders. He just whistled low, and quietly mopped his brow. The Daisy Bradford 3 was a spouting oil well. It was one of the three most significant days in the history of petroleum. Oil Creek, August 27, 1859; Spindletop, January 10, 1901; and now, East Texas, October 3, 1930.

As oil discoveries go, the Daisy Bradford 3 was not considered sensational. Those who had condemned the area as an oil prospect rationalized but still they were puzzled. Maybe there was a pimple of a structure on the Bradford farm. Maybe this and maybe that. There wasn't anything much said about the well for a few days. Three days later, in a short news item on the sports page of the *Dallas News*, a report simply said the well was flowing "by heads" every two hours making fifty-two barrels of oil in seventeen minutes at its longest spurt. On that basis, the story said, it was capable of a daily production of 5600 barrels.

No one knew it then, but the conflagration had been kindled. It was slow getting started, but two months later

Ed W. Bateman's well on the Lou Della Crim farm near Kilgore, twelve miles north of the Bradford farm, blew in from the same Woodbine sand making 22,000 barrels a day. Then Deep Rock Oil brought in another well a mile west of the Bradford farm with better pressure and the same sand. But the big break came when Farrel-Moncrief and Arkansas Fuel Oil's well came in on the Lathrop farm fifteen miles north of the Lou Della Crim and twenty-seven miles north of the Joiner discovery, also in Woodbine.

For a few weeks oilmen believed there were three different fields. It was not conceivable that one unbroken oil sand stretched twenty-seven miles. Then wells started coming in between the three. Derricks went up like the pine trees they were hewn from, and each one was like a new spark in a field of dry grass. Before anyone knew what was happening, a whole countryside was ablaze. Every day brought a new boom somewhere along the ten-mile-wide strip of Woodbine that nestled along almost sixty miles of the west side of the Sabine uplift.

Before anyone could stop to survey what was happening, East Texas was all of the oil booms in the world rolled into one. It was Oil Creek and Spindletop and El Dorado, Greater Seminole and Burkburnett, Glenn Pool and Signal Hill, Ranger and Desdemona, all in one great fairway. The Great Black Giant of the oil empire was striking with a fury that swept away the ills of economic depression for the poor people of East Texas.

The little parcels of land from which the poor whites and the Negroes of East Texas had barely eked out livings with skimpy crops of cotton, sweet potatoes and yellow corn, were soon one great patchwork quilt of leases stretching over four counties and 150,000 acres.

Pipelines and gathering systems grew like an enormous spider web. Oil was moving to markets by truck and tank cars and even an occasional horse-drawn wagon loaded with barrels. The countryside was permeated with the odor of hydrocarbons, foul to an outsider's senses, but sweeter than the perfume of Tyler's fragrant roses in festival time to the East Texans. Refineries and tanks glistened in the brilliant Southern sun.

The days passed and the poor became well-to-do, the well-to-do became wealthy and the wealthy grew richer. Dirt farmers were caught up in a maelstrom of leasing, selling and trading. Men who never had more than a few dollars in their pockets at one time were wearing store-bought suits and putting small fortunes in the new banks that were opening every day in an area around which other banks were closing almost as fast.

Around the Bradford farm a town grew up and they called it Joinerville. Soon the dust and cobwebs of New London, Overton and Kilgore were swept away, and the vacant lots filled up with towering obelisks over oil wells. Stores and barbershops and frame office buildings were demolished to make room for wells. On the outer fringes of the town new stores and shops and offices appeared. Old houses gave way to new brick residences, and out along the country lanes mansions replaced old farm-houses.

East Texas became the land of the prodigal son. When the word of the boom broke upon the depression-stricken country, young people who had left the parched acres of the poor lands to seek a better life, started trooping home again to help the old folks count their fortunes.

The evils of all of the oil booms were there in proper proportion. It was like a world convention of gamblers, prostitutes and confidence men held in a God-fearing country of hard-shelled Baptists and shouting 'Postolics. But the protests and pleadings of the preachers and their good people were drowned out by louder shouts of "Oil—more oil!"

Shyster lawyers, two-bit politicians and bootleggers and other home-grown scalawags came into their own. Their unprincipled double-dealing gained for them positions of wealth and power. They cheated and connived in leases and royalties, beating the gullible farmers out of fortunes and their croplands. They framed, maligned and even plotted the murder of those bold enough to stand up for their own rights.

This was not a single boom town. It was a whole countryside and dozens of towns and hamlets on fire with the excitement of liquid gold. The glory road led through Tyler, Henderson, Longview, Kilgore, and Gladewater, the latter two towns being right in the field itself. They all grew from whistle stops into thriving cities. The great rush of activity spread west to Dallas and Fort Worth, north to Oklahoma City and Tulsa, east to Shreveport and Baton Rouge, and south to New Orleans and Houston. Nowhere in that vast area was the Great Depression causing anywhere near the misery it was spreading to other parts of the nations.

Within a few months the chaos and confusion of the wild orgy of drilling started to backfire. In August of

1931 there was a period during which a million barrels of oil were coming out of the Woodbine blanket every day. By October a well was being completed every hour. The oil men appealed to the state for help. The landowners, businessmen and finally all of the people saw their great Black Giant forming itself into a Frankenstein monster that would devour and destroy the goodness it had brought them.

The Texas Railroad Commission, charged by law with the regulation of the oil industry in that state, twiddled its thumbs until the spring of 1931 without taking a step to control the field. Then it was too late for ordinary action. The complications of curtailment were more than the three weary politicians on the commission could cope with. First the commission ordered production held to 70,000 barrels a day, but by the time the order was issued the field was already flowing twice that much. Then the commission ordered the field cut back to 90,000 barrels a day, only to find production was over 300,000 barrels a day. By June 1 there were 1000 wells in the field, and the commission again ordered a cutback, this time to 160,000 barrels. But by then 400,000 barrels were coming out of the ground each day and no one cut back. The commission had no way of enforcing its orders.

With each new day and each new well the price of oil declined. The operators had to produce more oil to keep their incomes on an even keel, and the more oil they produced the lower prices fell. Oilmen were producing themselves into destruction. A confused legislature pondered the problem and fumbled. The governor sought an answer but his efforts were like fighting the wind with a fishing net. The commission issued orders, and the courts enjoined the orders.

And still more wells came in. There were no dry holes. Only mechanical breakdowns caused wells to fail. This was a carnival of oil production. While elsewhere the economic forces had been stilled by depression, East Texas was a mad and devastating oil boom. Little farms were deserted and leased, and the lessees subdivided them and leased the small plots. Thousands of one-acre tracts were being traded and drilled.

Pleas and threats and violence failed to hold back the cascade of oil that kept pouring onto the gently rolling hills and valleys of East Texas.

On August 15 Governor Ross Sterling ordered 1300 cavalrymen of the Texas National Guard into the field to enforce the orders of the Railroad Commission and the attorney general. By then the average production was 850,000 barrels of oil daily. Production was arbitrarily stopped until order could be restored and some kind of equitable proration plan could be worked out. Drilling went forward even though oil could not be taken from the wells.

But the governor was dealing with what operators considered their private property. He was himself a former president of the Humble Oil and Refining Company, a Standard Oil of New Jersey affiliate; and the commanding officer of the National Guard was General Jacob Wolters, whose civilian occupation had been as attorney for The Texas Company. Immediately several small operators protested that they were being taken in by a conspiracy of the big companies. On October 13 the federal court decided that the National Guard had no authority to enforce Railroad Commission orders. The governor then supplanted the orders of the Commission with his own to enforce proration.

The first proration order permitted wells to produce 185 barrels a day with overall production set at 400,000 barrels a day. But as the number of producers increased it was necessary to cut individual well allowables back to avoid exceeding the top allowable that engineers said was the maximum beyond which physical waste would result.

The situation in East Texas went from bad to worse and, in spite of the governor's troops, hot oil came into existence. That was oil produced in excess of allowables which by-passed the official count one way or another. By the end of 1931 there were almost 4000 wells in the field, enough for forty normal oil booms. On the day Dad Joiner's little well started flowing by heads down on the Daisy Bradford Farm, oil was worth $1.10 a barrel. Before proration East Texas oil was down to as low as ten cents, mid-continent oil was down to fifteen cents, and other oil prices throughout the world were depressed in proportion.

The East Texas field became a mecca for oilmen throughout the nation. Governor "Alfalfa Bill" Murray shut down the Oklahoma City and Greater Seminole fields in Oklahoma until, he said, the price of oil again reached a dollar. In other areas they didn't need a governor to shut down fields. The prices did that, and other oil men rushed to East Texas. By January, 1932, there were 600 American oil fields closed down.

The oracles of oil began to sound the notes of doom. This field was ruining the industry. There was no way to stop it, especially when it became apparent that the second federal case against the governor was bound to succeed. One operator had contended that martial law was illegal under any circumstances in East Texas since there had been no insurrection. If the court agreed there would be little control of the field. The frenzied drilling and selling and stealing and waste would break out again.

On December 12 the order was handed down. General Wolters' authority ended. The governor's orders were nullified. The governor himself had been defeated at the polls by "Ma" Ferguson, and his efforts to stabilize East Texas had been largely responsible. The day was one of the darkest in the history of petroleum. The captains of the oil industry braced themselves for the shock of destruction. One operator in federal court had handcuffed a governor and his army and in doing so had jeopardized the industry, the economy of the state and the entire oil country.

Back in June, Pat Neff, a former governor of the state, had resigned from the Railroad Commission to accept the presidency of Baylor University. Ross Sterling had immediately appointed Colonel Ernest O. Thompson, a young political Lochinvar out of the Panhandle, to fill out the four years left to the six-year term. The Railroad Commission being an elective position, Thompson could serve only until a successor to Neff was elected. He could serve by appointment until January 1, but he also had to announce his candidacy in the Democratic Party primary immediately. While the other two commissioners, old and weary of the unrelenting battle of lawsuits, orders and injunctions, had been carrying on, Thompson had been spending much of his time in a hard campaign to hold the job.

He had given little time to the paramount problems of the Commission. For a few weeks he had, however, boned up on the situation with a view toward a task he had been selected to accomplish.

With martial law ending in November, the Commission would have to enforce its own orders and regulations. Lon A. Smith and Judge C. V. Terrell, the other two commissioners, had suggested that Thompson move to Kilgore and take over. He had readily accepted the challenge.

It was noon of December 12. General Jacob Wolters' authority had expired. Thompson, called Colonel by his friends out of deference to a brilliant war record which included his becoming a lieutenant colonel in a battlefield promotion, was in a small pyramidal tent on a hill just outside Kilgore to take over his duties.

The colonel, a man of medium build, was crowned with a head of the reddest hair that three generations of Texans could produce. His wit was as lively as the twinkle in his eyes, but his manner was one of imperturbability and self-assurance. He displayed no fear or even dissatisfaction at the assignment in spite of his lack of experience.

General Wolters, tired and disgusted with the whole unpleasant job that he had been carrying out and the severe and continuous criticism that had gone with it, pondered his successor and wondered how long the colonel's present high spirits and good humor would last.

There was no ceremony. The colonel asked General Wolters what name he had for his headquarters. The general replied that he had frequently considered calling it hell, but that he hadn't taken the step publicly yet.

"It is probably the same thing in more words," the colonel smiled, "but if you have no objections, sir, I'll call it Proration Hill." The title fit, and the general was amused at the younger man's sense of humor.

"You just sign that memorandum receipt and you can have your hill and proration, too," Wolters replied. The receipt was for government equipment, including tents, horses, and guns for the 112th Cavalry Brigade of the Texas National Guard. The governor had agreed to leave a few troopers there until the Commission could replace them with its own enforcement team.

The informal transfer over, the colonel settled into his canvas chair and surveyed his battlefield as it appeared from under the tent flaps on all four sides. Wherever he looked there were oil derricks and rushing people and vehicles. He recalled a geologist saying that most of the oil produced was from one hundred million to a half-billion years old. Here was a national resource that was bringing progress and prosperity to a young nation, and it was being wasted as if it were salt water on an ocean beach.

"You know, sergeant," Thompson said to a clerk in his tent, "somebody is going to have to take hold of this thing right and it looks like I have been elected."

Even as he spoke, the operators of confusion were saying: "Who is this redhead from Amarillo, and how can he lick a problem that has stumped the governor, the legislature, the attorney general, and the National Guard?"

Their questions would be answered soon and decisively.

CHAPTER II

Amarillo Redhead

A round-faced boy with red hair and freckles sat huddled by the heater in the Amarillo depot. Outside it was near-zero weather and still dark. Ernest Thompson hadn't thawed out from the ride to the station and his eyes were still full of sleep.

Then he heard the low, distant whistle of the Fort Worth and Denver local. It was almost 4:30, and the mournful sound was the alarm that fully awakened him as it did every morning of the week, including Sundays. The train puffed to a squeaking stop as steam from the big locomotive's boilers vaporized above the station platform.

"Here you are, Ernest," shouted a cheerful baggage-man as he tossed off three bundles of papers. The boy waved a greeting and smiled at the man in the big open door. He picked up his bundles and went back into the waiting room where he sorted out the *Fort Worth Record*, the *Dallas News*, and the *St. Louis Post-Dispatch* for delivery. Then he threw the double bag over his pony's croup and was off on his route.

Within an hour his work was finished and he was back at home starting a fire in the stove and putting on the

16

coffee for the rest of the family. Soon his mother was awake and a hot breakfast was on the table. Then Ernest went back to town and sold the papers he had left from his route. His beat was the cowboy saloons and the other dives along Amarillo's Bowery section of 1903. He usually finished his job in time to get to school before the other kids and have a long play period before the first bell rang.

That was the boy Ernest Othmer Thompson, eleven years old and son of Amarillo's only druggist, Lewis Oliver Thompson, in the days when the metropolis of the Texas Panhandle had a population of hardly more than 1500 citizens, most of whom had come to the territory since the railroad was built through the town.

Ernest was born in Alvord, a small town in Wise County in North Central Texas which was distinguished only by its being on the route of the old Butterfield stage, the government telegraph line, and the Chisholm trail along which cattlemen drove their herds from the south to the markets in Abilene and points north.

L. O. Thompson settled in Alvord in the early 80's when he came out of the high plains country with his four brothers. All of them had been cowpunchers in the Tascosa Country, the cowboy capital of the Texas Panhandle on the Canadian River, and the home of the famous Boot Hill cemetery. In 1889 the Fort Worth and Denver opened the country up between the two towns that bore the name of the road, directly through the great plains country, and L. O. Thompson decided he would some day return to the land of his cowpunching days. In 1902 he did.

Ernest's mother, Flora Lee Murray Thompson, who was also born in Texas, was a woman of strong character and indomitable spirit. She was a good mother and devoted to her Presbyterian faith. There were two more boys and a girl in the family by the time the Thompsons arrived in Amarillo. One girl had died in infancy.

L. O. Thompson was not a poor man, and Ernest was neither forced nor encouraged to work. He was allowed to make his own decision. "If the boy wants to work, it'll be good for him," he told Lee when she complained that L. O. was too hard on the boy. Before he started a newspaper route, Ernest and his brothers worked in the Thompson drug store. Mr. Thompson let them wait on customers even when they had to stand on a stool to see over the glass showcases. The boys regarded that as fun and a privilege. That was how they got their first lessons in responsibility.

When he was a small boy a friend offered to trade a gun, that Ernest wanted very much, for a goat and harness which his father had given him. The boy approached Mr. Thompson and told him about the proposed trade. Mr. Thompson didn't tell Ernest that what he proposed was a bad trade. He decided to let the boy find out for himself.

"Ernest," he said, "that goat is yours. You can trade it if you want to, but before you decide, why don't you go down town and find out what the goat will bring you in money. And go to the harness maker; he'll tell you what the harness is worth, too. Then make your own decision."

Ernest followed his father's suggestion and found out

that the goat and harness were worth three guns. He wanted the gun, so he made the trade anyway, but he got five dollars cash in the bargain.

That was L. O. Thompson's way. He didn't order the boys to do anything. He didn't forbid anything. His way was to let them find out the facts for themselves, analyze their problems and make their own decisions. That's how Ernest became a newspaper carrier. He looked into the possibilities and his father told him to make up his own mind. It meant getting up early and working hard while the rest of the family slept. Ernest decided it was a chance for him to have his own business and earn his own money and that appealed to him.

It wasn't too long until Ernest had built his route up to the point that he had to hire another boy to work for him. Then he took on a second and a third boy and became an agent in his own right, with routes all over town. Finally, he put a newsstand in the Thompson drug store, and the business did so well that he was able to sell it for $150. The new boy lost interest and let the routes and the stand run down. Ernest had to take over again. Twice more he sold the business, and twice more they were returned to him when his successors failed to produce as Ernest did. He was a friendly boy and he knew every single one of Amarillo's 1500 inhabitants. As the town began to expand he met almost every newcomer and made a customer of him.

One of his toughest assignments was a customer who lived a mile off his route down a country lane. Ernest wanted to stop service to him, but Mr. Thompson put his foot down.

"Ernest, that man is a customer," he said, "and you keep right on throwing that paper, rain or shine."

The boy didn't like it but he followed his father's suggestion. He threw the paper on the roof, in bushes and, when it rained, in the biggest mud puddle he could find, to invite cancellation. But the customer liked Ernest and he never stopped the paper. And Ernest kept throwing it. When he decided there was no way to get the man to complain, he started hitting the porch again.

By the time he was in high school Ernest had more than $900 he had made and saved. With that he put a concession stand in the opera house and hired a man to run it while he went to school. He sold that at another $150 profit in three months and bought a drug store for $3000, most of which he was able to borrow on his own promise to repay. In another three months he sold the drug store at $1000 profit. He had more than $2000 in the bank, with his note paid.

It was 1908, and the Panhandle was beginning to expand by leaps and bounds. By that year Amarillo had grown to a city of 10,000, with Middle Westerners swarming down in search of farm lands on this great fertile plain. Frequently these newcomers came to look over the situation in advance of actually moving. Every other Friday a big excursion arrived in Amarillo with homeseekers. Ernest bought a large, seven-passenger Pope-Toledo town car and hired out himself and his car twice a month to a real-estate dealer to show boomers the country around Amarillo over the week-ends. The teachers complained of his missing school every second Friday, but the boy was making more on those afternoons than the teachers were making in a month, so their pleadings didn't make sense to him. His only penalty, and he didn't regret it because he was only sixteen, was spending an extra year in high school to complete his neglected math course.

It was in the summer between his fourth year in high school and the extra year that he made a deal with J. J. Curry, a local automobile enthusiast, to go to New York and buy forty second-hand Pope-Toledos to resell in Amarillo. Ernest took care of most of the details himself and split the profits with Curry. They polished the old, double-chain-drive, seven-passenger monsters, and put them in good running order. With each car Ernest gave driving lessons, since few people had mastered the art. In almost every case he had to take in a horse as a trade-in. But he protected himself there, too. He made a deal with John McKnight, the livery-stable owner who knew every horse in town, and got an estimate on the trade-ins before each deal. The trade-in allowance was exactly what McKnight said he would pay Ernest for a horse.

Ernest Thompson at eighteen was a prosperous and successful businessman. When he finished high school in 1910 he boarded a train for Indianapolis and obtained the franchise to sell Overland automobiles throughout the Panhandle area. That summer he sold ninety-two Overlands. They cost $960 without windshields, mud-guards or headlights, and $1100 with these "extras." With the money he had earned he decided to get a military education. Outside of West Point there was no better place for that than the Virginia Military Institute in Lexington. His interest in the military stemmed from another sideline he adopted as a boy. For several years he was the mascot, and at seventeen a member, of the Amarillo National Guard Company and had attended the summer encampments. The life appealed to him and he entered VMI with the determination to become a great general some day. He withstood the unmerciful hazing and was one of the campus favorites when disaster struck. An epidemic of pinkeye hit Lexington, and VMI was closed in the spring. It was then that he decided he might make an even better businessman than a soldier. He enrolled in Eastman's business college in Poughkeepsie, New York and sailed through the six-months course in half of that time. One thing he learned there was shorthand. The other was that there was nothing wrong with his previous business training.

Young Ernest went home to make further plans for an education. After a talk with his mother he decided to enroll in Texas University and become a lawyer. In the midst of his plans for this, however, he received a letter from an old acquaintance, John M. Willys of Elmira, New York. Willys was a bicycle dealer who had handled Overlands and whom Ernest had met on occasions at the factory.

Willys wanted to purchase the Overland factory, which was not doing so well at the time, and he wanted Ernest Thompson for a partner. Ernest came to the conclusion that he could not get an education if he went into the business, so he declined in spite of the fact that Mr. Willys had offered to make all financial arrangements. He told Willys of his plans and Willys came back with another proposition.

"Work for me while I'm getting started and I'll pay you $5000 and all expenses, which will be enough to completely finance your college education. You are still young," he wrote, "and the remainder of this year out of school will eliminate all worry about eventually finishing. You can still enroll at the start of next year's college term."

Making his own decision as L. O. Thompson had taught him, Ernest accepted. For a year he worked the territory of Indiana, Tennessee, Ohio, Kentucky, western New York, and western Pennsylvania for Willys. And in that period of time he disposed of 2010 Willys-Overlands. When the year was up Willys sent the young man nine cars on consignment to sell around Austin at a profit sufficient to pay for his first year of college.

The fall of 1912 Ernest Thompson, still under twenty years of age, enrolled in the University of Texas. In the bank he had enough money to see him through law school. Every cent of it had been earned by his own work. While L. O. Thompson, now a successful wholesale druggist, would have proudly paid the boy's way through college, Ernest preferred to use his own money rather than save it to set himself up in practice. That way he knew he would study more seriously and accomplish more for himself as a man. Lee Thompson still believed the method was a little severe, but she acquiesced because nothing but good had come from L. O.'s methods up to then.

Ernest pledged Phi Kappa Phi fraternity and took on the job of steward in the fraternity house. It was his idea to make the dollars he had in the bank last as long as possible. He was thinking ahead to the day when he got his degree and put up a shingle in Amarillo. Those years would be hard. His job would take care of his room and board.

One of the traits of Ernest Thompson that was to live with him through his life was his self-confidence. He never had the slightest doubt that he could accomplish anything he set out to do. Somewhere in his experience he had noticed an inclination on the part of most young men to do less than they were capable of accomplishing. He believed firmly that such a situation worked to his advantage because it removed a major portion of the competition. His own accomplishments had all come through a combination of hard work and a search for the facts in anything that he undertook. To a wise father and frugal Scotch mother he owed a great deal.

He entered the University with the same enthusiasm with which he had entered his work on the newspaper route, his confectionery, the drug store, the automobile business and his school work back in Amarillo. He had acquired an interest in life that would never be completely satisfied, and his thoughts that September morning as he walked down Congress Avenue were far in the future. Or were until a large black car whisked by and snapped him out of his dreams. It was so new he could smell the paint. He wheeled around and saw it turn into Fifth Street and pull up in front of the Driskill Hotel. Ernest Thompson didn't know what it was that caused him to follow the big car, but that seeming trifle was to change the course of his whole life.

CHAPTER III

Ernest and the Judge

Parke Houston was a little puzzled by Ernest Thompson's line of questioning. The young man had followed the big black limousine around the corner and had stopped Houston as he was about to drive away from the Driskill Hotel.

Houston had assured Ernest that he was not a chauffeur, and that the elderly man in the derby hat and the well-dressed woman with him were not the owners of the automobile.

"That was Judge Gaines and his wife," Houston explained. "I am a salesman for the Rex Thomson Pierce Arrow Company and I have been demonstrating this car with the hope of selling it to them."

"It certainly is a fine motorcar," Ernest said. "I'm glad to know that you are not interested in being a chauffeur. I would like to have the job of driving this machine and if you don't mind, I'll take it up with Mr. Thomson."

Parke Houston didn't mind.

Ernest Thompson stood for a few minutes watching the big 66 Pierce Arrow as it cruised down the street. Then he walked back to Congress Avenue and turned left two blocks to the Rex Thomson storeroom.

"Mr. Thomson, I'm Ernest Thompson from Amarillo. I was in the automobile business until a few months ago and now I am enrolled in the University here," Ernest explained to Rex Thomson as he extended his hand in introduction.

The Pierce Arrow dealer was a bit skeptical that this boy, who was still under twenty and looked even younger, had been an automobile dealer. But he heard the whole story and was impressed.

Then Ernest put his proposition. "I would like to have a spare-time job driving that car. If you will help me get the job of chauffeur, I'll help you sell the car to Judge Gaines," he said. Rex Thomson agreed. Ernest didn't ask for a commission. He did say, however, that he would be competing with himself since he had a few cars left which he was trying to sell in Austin.

Ten minutes after he left Thomson, Ernest was rapping on the Gaines suite in the Driskill. When Mrs. Gaines came to the door, the young man introduced himself and asked if he might see the judge.

Within a half hour Judge and Mrs. Gaines had heard the story of how Ernest first saw the car, his natural interest in fine automobiles, and that he would like to apply for the part-time job of driving it, if the judge bought the car.

Ernest then related his experience with automobiles. He told how he had driven on week-ends for the home-seekers in the Panhandle, how he had sold cars and then managed his own garage. The judge was convinced that if anyone could drive a car this young man could.

"Well, we are thinking seriously of buying the car and

we will need a driver," Judge Gaines said. "By the way, are you acquainted with the lawyers in the Panhandle, Judges Kimbrough, Trulove and Madden?" he asked.

After Ernest assured the judge that he knew the three men intimately, Judge Gaines suggested that Ernest prepare a telegram for Gaines's signature asking recommendations.

"If your recommendations come through, you ask Rex Thomson to let you demonstrate your driving ability and the car again tomorrow and if everything is right, you can have the job," Judge Gaines said. "How much do you think I should pay you?"

The question caught Ernest a little short. "Why, Judge, I'd almost work for nothing just to drive that car," he smiled.

The next day the replies to the telegrams came. Neither Ernest nor Judge Gaines had any doubt about them, and the judge didn't tell Ernest what they said. But that afternoon Ernest demonstrated both his prowess behind the wheel and many things about the car that others had not shown the judge and his wife.

The salary was agreed to. It would be $50 a month. Ernest was instructed to pick up the car each afternoon at four o'clock when the judge left his office, and to be available for night and week-end visits. As Ernest handed Rex Thomson a check for $5600 for the automobile, he said with a satisfied smile, "I guess I won't need any help to get that job, Mr. Thomson."

As the weeks passed Ernest endeared himself to both Judge and Mrs. Gaines. Back in Amarillo Ernest's parents were delighted that their son was in the employ of such people and was with them most of the time he was not actually in classes. To Ernest the Gaineses were almost like parents.

Judge Gaines had learned in conversations with Ernest that he had completed a shorthand and typing course at Eastman school. One afternoon on the way home he made Ernest a proposition. He proposed that a room be added to the Gaines suite in the Driskill and that Ernest move in to become the judge's private secretary and handle Mrs. Gaines's business affairs as well.

At first Ernest protested that he could not afford a room in the hotel. The judge told him that he had no intention of Ernest's paying for the room. In fact the judge would pay for the room, meals and laundry and still pay the boy $50 a month. A colored boy that both Judge Gaines and Ernest liked very much could be trained to drive the car.

It was a remarkable opportunity for Ernest, and he made his decision to accept the job immediately. The judge told him that the job would not be altogether a vacation since he had much after-work dictation— sometimes he would be waking Ernest up in the middle of the night to dictate ideas that came to him—but that he believed Ernest would enjoy the job. Ernest thought of the additional advantage of being close to the judge, who was one of the most renowned attorneys in Texas and who could help him considerably in his law studies.

Judge Reuben R. Gaines was a former member of the Texas Supreme Court. He was a native Alabamian who had been an adjutant in the Confederate army during the Civil War and had reached the rank of major. He was a most successful lawyer. Quiet and dignified in manner, he was a provident man of great foresight. The years that Ernest Thompson would spend with him would further prepare the young man for his tremendous task.

Each summer Ernest returned to his driving role and took the Judge and Mrs. Gaines on a long vacation trip. The first summer they went to Yosemite Park when it was opened for automobile traffic and the big Pierce Arrow was the second or third automobile to enter. Between Ernest's sophomore and junior years in the University, the three went to New England and spent almost three months in a cottage at Bass Rocks, Massachusetts. All of this time Ernest was free to listen to the judge impart his philosophy of life and his understanding of the constitution and the laws. A brilliant student, Ernest had done well in his college work preparing for law school, but the advantage of being constantly with one of the state's great jurists would later make him one of the most promising undergraduates of the school of law.

In his first three years in the University Ernest had been home only on Christmas, Thanksgiving or Easter holidays. He had never had time to spend a summer with his family. As the term closed in 1913 the judge called him into the living room of his suite one evening and said it was time to prepare for the summer trip.

"This year Mrs. Gaines and I are going to let you choose the place, Ernest," he said.

"Judge, I'm afraid I can't go this summer," Ernest replied rather reluctantly. He felt that he was needed on the trips since the judge was too old to drive himself.

Then he explained that he had not been home for three summers and that he wanted to visit his parents.

"That's fine," Judge Gaines said. "We'll all go to Amarillo. I want to visit some of my old friends there, anyway, and Mrs. Gaines and I think it's about time to meet the parents of our boy." Mrs. Gaines enthusiastically endorsed the plan.

It was a happy summer. The judge met the Thompsons and all of Ernest's many friends in Amarillo. The town was almost twice as large as it had been when Ernest left three years before but it seemed as if everyone there knew him or had heard about him.

The next year was Ernest's first in law school and he was immediately recognized as one of the leaders in the class. His tremendous vitality and drive kept him at the head of campus activities in spite of his duties with the judge almost every evening. Judge Gaines took an increasing interest in the young man as he went through the law course. The judge had received his basic schooling at Alabama University but had gone to Cumberland for his law degree. He told Ernest that the advantages at Texas were much greater and he predicted that the energetic redhead would become a great lawyer if business didn't steal him away from the profession.

As the later part of May, 1914, came around Judge Gaines seemed to have some kind of premonition. He had wanted to make a trip to Europe all his life and now he had decided to do it.

"Ernest," he called from the parlor of his suite one evening, "how would you like to join Mrs. Gaines and me on a trip to Europe? It will be an education and we will be delighted to have you as a companion. In fact, without you, I doubt that we could go at all."

Ernest Thompson was elated. He accepted immediately and then went to the telephone to call his parents and tell them the good news. That night the three stayed up far beyond their normal bedtime planning an itinerary. They would start in Italy to get the benefit of a Mediterranean cruise and then go to Switzerland, Austria, France, Germany, Holland, and possibly England and Ireland. Ernest said he might take a side trip into Scotland to see the land of his ancestors.

Early the next morning Judge Gaines gave Ernest some instructions that he would never forget.

First, he told him to go to a travel agency and make reservations on a liner and to plan to ship the car ahead of time. He was also to find out the name of a hotel in every town on the long itinerary made out the evening before and make reservations for each night of the entire trip. He was told to check, first, the highway conditions to be certain there were good roads—good enough for the Pierce Arrow—and, if any flaws were found, to change the itinerary accordingly. Then, the judge said, get confirmations on each reservation. "Leave no detail undone, Ernest," he warned. "We want to have a pleasant trip. Let's take all of the trouble now and enjoy Europe."

Ernest knew how to plan. The judge had taught him much in the four years. With all of his work done and a full notebook of data on towns and hotels and customs, Ernest reported back to the judge.

"Now, Ernest, I think we will need some money," the

judge said. "Go down to the bank and purchase $2500 in American Express traveler's checks, then purchase another $2500 in German checks. When you get through with that go down to the saddle shop and have a good money belt made, one you can wear around your waist. Then take it to the Austin National Bank and fill it with as many $20 gold pieces as you can carry comfortably on your person. If everything else fails, we will have that to fall back on."

Ernest marveled at this man of meticulous detail who anticipated every eventuality and took the necessary precautions. Ernest thought possibly he was a little too exacting, but he followed the instructions to the letter.

Probably the most important single incident of the trip to Naples for Ernest Thompson was his daily walks on the ship's deck with Cardinal Gibbons. It started one day as Ernest and the judge were reclining in steamer chairs outside the Gaines cabin.

"You see that man, Ernest," Judge Gaines said pointing to a thin man with gray hair dressed in a priest's hassock. "That is James Cardinal Gibbons, one of the great Americans. You should introduce yourself to him."

Ernest walked over to the cardinal and presented himself. A few minutes later the two were back talking with Judge and Mrs. Gaines. The judge filled the cardinal in on Ernest and the churchman was impressed. He invited Ernest to accompany him on his daily walks around the deck, which Ernest accepted with pride. Thereafter the daily date with the cardinal was the prime event of the voyage and the two talked at great length about many things. The cardinal, who had been a chaplain with the Union army during the Civil War, was a great advocate of the American principle of separation of church and state. He had defended the Knights of Labor after a Canadian cardinal had attacked the organization. His loves were his church and his country. Ernest listened and learned from the great churchman, nearly seventy-five years old and making his last trip to the Vatican.

When the ship docked in Naples the Pierce Arrow was there just as the judge had instructed and as Ernest had ordered. It was filled with fuel and ready to go. Their first weeks were spent in Naples, Rome and other Italian cities. Everywhere the advance planning paid off well. There was never any bother or confusion. Every detail was as the judge had planned and Ernest had ordered.

On the morning of June 29 the small Texas party was in Meran, Austria in the Tyrolean Alps. Ernest was looking over the morning paper to improve his ability to read German when one item caught his attention. He read it to the judge.

"It says here that Franz Ferdinand, the heir apparent to the Austrian throne, and the Duchess of Hohenberg, his morganatic wife, were assassinated yesterday in Sarajevo by Gario Princip, a student, with an automatic pistol," Ernest read.

"Read that again," Judge Gaines said as he put his coffee down on the table. Ernest read the item again very carefully and deliberately. Then he added, "The bodies are being sent back to Vienna for a state funeral."

Judge Gaines suggested that they cancel the next week's reservations immediately and go to Vienna. "Get us a room in a hotel overlooking the Ringstrasse where we will be able to see the funeral procession, Ernest," the judge said. "This will be an occasion that will go down in history and one that you must not miss, son."

On the second day after that Judge and Mrs. Gaines and Ernest were in a room in the leading hotel in Vienna, overlooking the Ringstrasse. On the day of the funeral procession they had ringside seats. Right beneath their window passed the bodies of the slain couple. Franz Josef, the Emperor of Austria-Hungary, led the cortege. The solemn procession, the weeping of the people, and the realization of the sorrow of the Hapsburgs impressed Ernest tremendously.

Shortly thereafter Ernest told Judge Gaines that he had read about the Austrian and Italian soldiers massing for maneuvers. When the Austrians demanded Princip for trial, the judge said that was a signal to get out of there as he saw the possibilities of trouble under these conditions of long pent-up hatreds.

The three Texans left Vienna and decided to pick up their planned itinerary with the reservations in Lucerne. They saw the hundreds of thousands of troops massed on both sides of the border in Austria and Italy. Passage was slow and tedious, but it was also interesting. In Switzerland they found the Swiss, too, were mobilizing. Uniforms were hanging out to air behind every Swiss home.

During their next three weeks in Lucerne the world moved steadily in the direction of Armageddon. On

July 28, one month to the day after the assassination, Austria declared war on Serbia. By that time the demand on American Express checks had been so great that the company's funds were exhausted, although a special cruiser was said to be bringing additional funds. On August 2, when Germany started to move on France through Luxemburg, the German notes became value-less, so the $20 gold pieces, the judge's ace-in-the-hole, proved the value of careful planning.

During the first week in August, with France under attack by the Germans, Judge Gaines sent Ernest to Paris to see what the situation was and to confirm their reservations, if he thought it safe enough. Ernest didn't cherish the train ride. No one had tickets; every seat and cab was filled. There was sadness in the air with people trying to get home. Men were rushing to Paris to help defend their country. Mothers and wives were rushing home to their men.

When he arrived in Paris the city was under complete blackout conditions but Ernest finally found the George V Hotel where he remained several days making reservations.

Back in Lucerne after another hectic train trip, Ernest and the judge loaded the old car with gasoline and provisions, including two spare tires. Several cans of gasoline were put in the back seat to ride with Mrs. Gaines. Then they were off for Paris and the war. When they arrived at the Swiss border they were stopped. The border patrol relieved them of their gasoline and spare tires which by that time had been placed on the country's critical list. They returned to Lucerne only to have the automobile confiscated. The judge decided they would go on to France by train. As little as he relished the ride again, Ernest was glad to get back to Paris where it would be relatively easy to get out of the country and back to America.

The Paris visit, however, was longer than he bargained for. Six sailings the judge had made were canceled. Every day the German advance brought the war closer to Paris. The cannonading could be heard all day; and at night the lights of battle could be seen from the hotel room, bursting on the northern horizon.

One day Ernest went down to the offices of the French Line again. Crowds were swarming in front of the building. Ernest, the cocksure, walked up to the guard on duty after pushing his way through the throng and said he must see the director. His manner was convincing. When the director came out Ernest suggested a number system to give each patron an equal chance instead of fighting for a place at the ticket counter. The system idea appealed to the official, and numbers from several old loose-leaf calendars were torn up and distributed. But while Ernest was behind the counter, an employee came in to announce a new sailing. Ernest seized the opportunity to line up space for his party.

From the window of the boat train Ernest saw the famous taxicab army assembling. At Le Havre, where the ship was waiting, he saw the Highland Guards debark from England—the "Ladies from Hell"—and before his ship sailed he saw the first battle casualties from that same brigade return to Le Havre for shipment back to England.

The trip back to America was on the ship of a belligerent and was fraught with danger. It was a tense trip in contrast with the remarkably peaceful and restful trip over. Most of the judge's plans had gone awry with the beginning of the great war, but his meticulous planning was a lesson Ernest would long remember.

Less than a month after the judge arrived back in Austin he became suddenly ill. He died in Ernest's arms.

CHAPTER IV

Machine Gunner

The death of Judge Gaines was a tremendous shock to
Ernest Thompson. The wise and kindly man had been
a father and a mentor to him. By the time he died, on
October 13, 1914, the war he had seen conceived was
beginning to engulf the world. He had fulfilled the
ambition of a lifetime to see Europe, but the excitement
that he had not bargained for, but had enjoyed, was
probably too much for his seventy-eight years.

Ernest was persuaded by Mrs. Gaines to continue
living in the hotel and to take care of her financial
affairs. That was quite a job, but it was far less than
Ernest had been accustomed to during the judge's
lifetime so that he had more time to devote to his classes
and the normal functions of being a student.

As the war rumbled on and it became more and
more obvious that the United States would become a
participant, some 1200 students at the University started
preparing for it. Those who like Ernest had had military
experience became instructors in the manual of arms,
marching, and care of the rifle. The dean of the law
school scoffed at the boys, saying he doubted if many of
them would become volunteers if war really came. How-

ever, the day that war was declared every man in the law class, except two, signed up for service. One of the exceptions was blind and the other had lost a leg in an accident. The law students, including Ernest, who was class president, left the University en masse and reported for duty at the first officers' training camp, at Leon Springs west of San Antonio. Their diplomas were delivered to them in June.

The training was rigorous. The camp had a quota of 1500 officers to commission, and there were 2500 eager and enthusiastic young Texans enrolled. At least a thousand of them would not become officers. Most of the 2500 were good officer material. It finally took long, forced marches with full packs to weed out almost half of the class on a physical-fitness basis.

Young Thompson took to military training as readily as he had taken to delivering a newspaper route or driving an automobile. His background stood him in good stead. His short time at VMI as a "rat," his days with the National Guard, his business training, and the fact that he knew this war from a first-hand impression at its very outset were all in his favor. His commanding officer, Captain Leslie J. McNair of the regular army, took great pride in the young man and made him his protégé. But McNair was not long for Leon Springs. General Pershing took him to France in the advance party of American troops as artillery officer.

McNair's old company was consolidated, when he departed, with another unit commanded by Colonel Charles F. Bates, a thirty-year man and a graduate of Harvard. A month before the camp closed Colonel

Bates enlisted Thompson to aid in classifying the other student officers. He assured Ernest he need not bother about further training as he had already been selected to become a captain. Ernest graded papers, made out questions and helped segregate the officers into compatible groups.

Thompson's company hit upon a novel idea shortly before the officers received their commissions. There was an army rule that a man could not be an officer and an enlisted man on the same day. Thompson suggested to Colonel Bates that the men be permitted to have a farewell dinner on the last night of their training at the Menger Hotel in San Antonio. At the termination of the dinner, a minute after midnight, Colonel Bates could present them with their commissions in a ceremony in front of the Alamo, next door to the Menger.

The colonel liked the idea for its dramatic possibilities and commissioned the company officers in the moonlight. Immediately after the ceremony the young men took off on the two-week leave they were entitled to before reporting for duty. The plan had worked. It gave them an extra day of leave, plus the newspaper stories.

Two weeks later the famous 90th Division was formed at Camp Travis in San Antonio with cadres of officers from Leon Springs. Captain Thompson became adjutant of the 358th Infantry regiment. Due largely to his interest in his work and also because he noticed that the colonels and generals seldom left the camp, Ernest usually found something to do there when the other young officers went on leave or to San Antonio for the evening. He had a feeling that most officers of his rank were equal in ability, but that if something good turned up in this period of building a division the man who happened to be present when opportunities came up would be chosen. His theory soon paid off. One evening he was called by the brigade commander, General Patsy O'Neal, a tremendous red-faced Irishman with bright-red whiskers, and offered the position of acting brigade adjutant, a position he lost no time in accepting.

In July the War Department ordered a machine-gun battalion formed in each brigade and an additional one in each division. The young brigade adjutant suggested that General O'Neal act immediately on the orders. The general agreed and left the organization plans to Thompson.

Machine guns appealed to Captain Thompson, and he believed the battalions should be elite units. His plan called for physically perfect specimens—at least six feet tall—among the enlisted men, and the best officers in the necessary grades from the two regiments in the brigade. It also provided that the limited arsenal of Lewis and Maxim machine guns (there were six of them in all) be turned over to the battalions. The Thompson plan was approved and the Camp Travis machine-gun battalions were the first in operation in the army. Captain Thompson was made acting commander of the 344th Machine Gun Battalion until the officer who was to be designated for the command returned from school at Fort Sill.

Within a few weeks, and before the other officer returned, the division was ordered overseas with Ernest getting a promotion to major and permanent command of the battalion. Within a few weeks after landing on

French soil the 90th Division was in action in the battle of the Argonne. During the battle Major Thompson was made division machine-gun officer on the staff of G3 at the request of General Henry T. Allen and his chief of staff, Colonel John J. Kingman.

Thompson's knack for machine-gun warfare was uncanny. He was soon recognized as one of the most proficient officers in the war in that particular arm. For months he planned machine-gun attacks, experimented and watched his plans mature.

It was during the Meuse-Argonne, the last battle of the war, that Ernest Thompson got the chance to prove his revolutionary machine-gun theories. The 90th Division was advancing toward the Meuse River in the fall of 1918 over a terrain that lent itself admirably to direct overhead machine-gun fire. It was an area where large hogback ridges lay on either side of a wide valley. The Germans had taken a defiant stand and had virtually stopped the Allied advance. The young major studied the situation from every angle. He made a clay model of the terrain from the excellent French military maps and came up with an idea for overcoming the withering fire of the Germans to permit the advance of the Allied troops.

He explained his plan to General Allen, proposing that the three division machine-gun battalions provide a curtain of fire over the heads of the advancing infantry, with French 75's behind the machine guns and 155 howitzers behind the 75's. He requisitioned 1,600,000 rounds of ammunition and 1000 ammunition carriers from each infantry regiment, since mules were too unreliable and too slow for the operation. In spite of the protests of the regimental commanders the orders were issued.

Thompson's plan pinpointed every machine-gun position in the entire barrage. Overlay maps not only showed the positions of the guns, but gave elevations and deflections. That information was given the machine gunners on cards to reduce error. As the great barrage started moving slowly forward on November 2, 1918, with a canopy of molten lead covering the advancing foot soldiers, the machine guns moved forward almost abreast. The long range 75's and the 155's remained stationary almost hub to hub.

The plan worked so perfectly that it was completed in less than a day's time, whereas four days had been allowed by the planning division for its complete execution. Thousands of resisting Germans were killed and more thousands surrendered as every objective was taken. The surrendering German officers were curious about the new secret weapon and were astounded to learn that it was nothing more than mass machine-gun fire.

A few days later General Pershing, on an inspection of the battle scene, one of the last of the war, informed Thompson through General Allen that he had been promoted to lieutenant colonel, the youngest man in the United States Army to attain that rank, for his battlefield excellence.

Within a few weeks the war ended with the 90th Division still on the banks of the Meuse. After the armistice Colonel Thompson was ordered into Germany to direct the massing of enemy arms, particularly machine guns and heavy artillery, although the German soldiers were permitted to keep their rifles.

In the occupation the division moved first into Bern-castle and then to Coblenz, where the Third Army was organized under General Allen's command. It was while in this occupation force that Thompson became one of the organizers of the American Legion. He was delegated by General Allen to go to Paris for the first caucus of the men who laid the groundwork for the organization. The Legion was not formed there since its organizers did not want to convey the impression that it was to be an overseas group. The formal organization was delayed a year and held later in St. Louis.

The colonel was requested to be a guest at the Peace Conference in Paris by Dr. Mezes, a former president of Texas University, who was there as assistant to Colonel E. M. House, the presidential adviser. He spent three weeks at the Conference and there made the acquaintance of Samuel Gompers, the father of American labor and an old friend of Cardinal Gibbons'. Thompson, in his typical manner, saw Gompers at breakfast one morning in the hotel and introduced himself. Thereafter the two men had breakfast together for six consecutive mornings and became fast friends.

His job accomplished in the great war, Thompson started looking for a way to get home. An order provided for officers in the forward occupation zone to exchange commands with officers of rear echelons of similar rank and qualifications who preferred occupation duty. The commanding officer of the 146th Infantry stationed at

Le Mans made such a trade with Thompson. It was a strange trade. Thompson borrowed a car to go to Le Mans to make the switch. The 146th commander merely asked Thompson if he were the exchange officer and then took over the car Thompson came in. There was no formal exchange of commands.

The regiment Thompson took over, however, was a big one and was billeted in fifteen different towns around Le Mans. But it was on schedule for return to the United States. The men were all from Ohio. The return trip home for Ernest Thompson was relatively uneventful except for one incident. He found a captain who had been a sophomore when he was a "rat" at VMI and who had been particularly unrelenting toward Ernest. As commander of troops on the ship, Ernest relegated his old tormentor to the lowest deck for the trip home. Once in New York, however, the two forgave each other for their respective abuses.

The 146th Infantry was mustered out of the service at Camp Sherman near Chillicothe, Ohio. The final banquet was at the armory at Akron. The principal speaker was ex-President William Howard Taft who had made a speech in San Antonio when the 90th Division was departing for France. Ernest reminded Taft of the San Antonio speech. When it came his turn for the address of the evening, Taft started by saying:

"Colonel Thompson has reminded me that I was the last public speaker he heard in this country at San Antonio when the 90th Division was leaving. He left America to keep from hearing me again. He bared his

45

breast to enemy fire as a preference. And now that he's home again, I am the first man he is to hear make a public speech."

The next day Ernest mustered out his troops and then took his own discharge to General Glenn for signature. The general proposed that he order Ernest to Fort Worth where he could be discharged, and thereby save his train fare for that much of the trip home.

"Thank you, general," Ernest smiled, "but if it's all right with you, just sign this discharge and I'll get home under my own steam. There might be some little job to do for the army around Fort Worth and it might take a year to do it."

The general understood the attitude of this citizen soldier and complied with his wish. Within a few hours Ernest Thompson was on his way back to old Rag Town beside the yellow waters of Amarillo Lake.

CHAPTER V

Mayor of Amarillo

The bands had quit playing for every boat that docked in New York from France by the time Ernest Thompson came home in 1919. Behind him were months in the Army of Occupation. And ahead was a future far more significant and almost as exciting as his adventurous past.

His return to Amarillo was auspicious enough. There was a reception for old Rag Town's hero whose machine-gun barrage had been described by General Pershing as one of the most meticulously planned and timed of the war and one of its truly decisive events. The *Amarillo News* carried a full interview with the youngest Lieutenant Colonel in the American Expeditionary Forces. It recalled his days as a newsboy, small businessman and big automobile dealer.

It was around the first of the year in 1920 before Colonel Thompson, as he was now generally known, had completed his library and hung a shingle out in front of his law office. Old friends and newcomers to Amarillo started beating a path to his door. He made $500 in his first month of practice, and the future looked brighter than ever. His townsmen had confidence and pride in him. His personal magnetism and charm were all-conquering.

One day H. P. Canode and his wife, Mary, owners of the old Amarillo Hotel, a rambling four-story frame structure built in 1889 and in which Ernest, the freckled-faced kid, had hawked newspapers, came to the new law office. They explained that they were getting old, wanted to retire, and had decided to sell the Amarillo for $200,000. They wanted Ernest to make the commission of $10,000 on the deal.

It was the first big deal that Ernest Thompson had been offered. He knew the hotel was worth the money in spite of its thirty-one years because the downtown lots alone were now highly valuable. He had no doubt about selling it within a few weeks.

The prospects, however, were all lukewarm. All except one, that is, who haggled for days over the price. Neither Ernest nor his client was willing to reduce the price and they soon became weary of the bickering. In the middle of a final sales talk, Ernest stopped short, motioned to Mr. Canode and his wife to follow him into the hall and excused himself from the prospect.

"Mr. Canode, this man is trying to beat the price down. I don't think he will pay the $200,000. I have just had a thought," Ernest said, "and I hope it appeals to you."

"Anything you say, Ernest, is all right with us," said Mr. Canode.

"Well, I have decided that you have a good deal and I will buy your hotel—if I can still get the commission on the sale," Ernest said. "I will have to raise the money, but if you will give me a ninety-day option, I'll get it."

Ernest got the option. He didn't need the ninety days. He had raised the money in one-tenth of that time for the first payment of $75,000, less his commission. Ernest Thompson was back in business before he realized it. He intended to practice law and live in the hotel to be near his business, but it didn't work. He fired one manager who had the idea that he could make a profit by reducing service and increasing prices. He fired a second manager because he couldn't get along with the employees. Then he found himself managing his own hotel. Under his supervision the business was soon booming. Rooms that hadn't been rented since the first day the place was opened were furnished and rented. The old shops were remodeled and the coffee shop and dining room were doing a thriving business. Within two years The Amarillo wasn't big enough for the town. The great Panhandle gas field was hit fifty miles north in 1921 and the boom was on. In 1922 The Amarillo was rebuilt into a modern concrete and steel twelve-story hotel, and still it was full. By this time Ernest had a reputation as a hotel operator and it was easy to get the financing he needed.

But as far as Ernest Othmer Thompson was concerned, the discovery of the Panhandle gas field was of secondary importance in 1921. That was the year that the "Golden Girl" of the Metropolitan Opera came to Amarillo to sing at the First Methodist Church. May Peterson was as lovely as she was talented and it didn't take the very sharp Mr. Thompson long to recognize that fact. He was selected by the civic committee as her escort since he was the town's outstanding eligible bachelor and most promising young attorney and businessman.

Never in his life before had the young colonel been so attracted to a young lady. He didn't have to tell her all about himself. His friends had done that. But Ernest was fascinated by the story of this fair daughter of a Methodist evangelist who had started singing at the age of four and had been fired with the ambition to become a great singer before she was out of her teens. She had become an English teacher in Europe to make enough money to study voice. Then she had gone to Italy and Germany to study. The way had been difficult. In Germany a companion had stolen all of her money and she had almost starved. Once, after days on bread and water, she had fainted from hunger on the streets of Berlin. By sheer determination she had managed to study under one of the great masters and even sing a command performance for the Kaiser. Her goal was the Opéra Comique of Paris and she had arrived there a year before the great war. She had studied under the famous Jean de Reszke in return for her services as his accompanist. During the hectic days of war training she had visited army camps in America. Before the end of the war her voice had led her right to the door of the Metropolitan where she signed a six-year contract in 1918. There she worked with Caruso and other immortals. But she always remained loyal to her church and sang benefit concerts in the off season. That's how she happened to be in Amarillo where the dashing young colonel was waiting for her.

For the next two years Ernest followed the glamorous

singer from one part of the country to another. It started
the night she closed the Amarillo concert. The next day
he went to Fort Worth for her concert. He was in St.
Louis for the organization meeting of the American
Legion when she was there. And when he was chosen to
represent Texas at the burial of the Unknown Soldier, he
had gone on to New York to hear her again and, of
course, to see her. By then the courtship was in full
flower.

In the meantime he had built the new Amarillo Hotel
and had started Amarillo's first multi-story office building, an eight-story structure designed for a future addition as large as the original.

In 1923 May Peterson was in Paris continuing her
voice lessons under de Reszke. That year Providence
arranged for Ernest to be chosen a delegate to the World
Congress of Allied Veterans in Brussels, a meeting of
combat veterans to outlaw war.

On the one day given over to rest, Ernest took a
train to Paris and persuaded May to return to Brussels
with him. The schedule the next day called for a reception by Queen Elisabeth, and Ernest had arranged with
his typical ingenuity to have May invited especially by
the Queen. May left the decision to Jean de Reszke and
he told her it would be unthinkable to refuse the invitation. Once in Brussels, Ernest prevailed on May to stay
for the final banquet two nights later. Again de Reszke
urged her to take the rest, which she sorely needed, from
her arduous work.

It was the afternoon before the great banquet and
Ernest took May to the Waterloo monument just south

of Brussels. There he displayed for a little while his knowledge of warfare by explaining the details of Wellington's defeat of Napoleon. Then came the moment for which he had planned.

"May, I want you to marry me as soon as we get back to New York," he said with just enough tenderness and the right amount of determination. "You have had my ring for a year, but you put it in your purse when you are around anyone except me. Say now that we can be married. On this ground Napoleon met his Waterloo. Here I am gambling as much as he did. Now tell me, who am I? Napoleon or Wellington?"

May Peterson slipped her arm into his and simply said: "It's about time to start dressing for the banquet isn't it——Wellington?"

That was the proposal and the acceptance. But Ernest felt that he must seal the promise. He took May to her room and rushed down the hall to the suite occupied by Edouard Herriot, the chairman of the Congress and the man who was to soon become the premier of France. Ernest talked briefly but eagerly to the great man and then left him. Herriot watched smilingly as the happy young Texan departed down the hall.

That evening, with all of the notables and the delegates gathered around the banquet table, Edouard Herriot arose to open the meeting.

"This conference has developed much, but nothing so important, I think, as a conquest of the heart," Herriot started with a broad smile. "The delegate from the United States, the distinguished colonel from Texas, Ernest Thompson, has won the lady of his heart. He and the lovely and most talented Miss May Peterson of the Metropolitan Opera are to be married upon their return to New York. I propose a toast to them."

May Peterson was stunned for a moment. She was not prepared for this surprise. Now she knew that the young redhead from Amarillo had truly sealed the bargain in his own way. There would be no backing out now. Every newspaper would have the story the next day, coming as it did from the lips of the French statesman on such an auspicious occasion.

Amarillo was never prouder of Ernest Thompson than it was the day he brought his beautiful bride home. He had won the hearts of his fellow townsmen all over again. May, the lovely and the talented, proved to be May, the gracious and popular in her adopted home town.

Through 1924 and 1925 Amarillo continued to expand. It became the center of an industrial area as well as of the cattle and wheat country. It became, too, a crossroads for the coast-to-coast travelers. In 1926 Colonel C. T. Herring told Ernest he was going to build a new hotel, finer than The Amarillo, which was bulging at its sides with business. "I think Amarillo needs a second hotel, but I think you should run it, too," he said. Before the new hotel opened, Ernest had a lease to operate it. In 1927 the hotel opened and it was an immediate success under the barrister-turned-innkeeper. The next year Ernest made arrangements with Colonel Herring to take over the new hotel. The colorful old colonel had what he wanted, a monument in brick and steel to carry his name. The hotel was called The Herring.

Governor Moody appointed Ernest to the Board of Regents at Texas Tech in 1928. And in that same year a campaign for mayor was on in Amarillo. There were three candidates, including the incumbent, and politics was beginning to warm up. As Ernest watched the campaign clouds gather he realized that Amarillo, a growing city, should have vigorous leadership. Somewhere in his bones the urge to politics had been born, and he decided to announce his candidacy. But his announcement was unique. "I own a lot of property in this town now," he said. "My taxes and my utility bills are as high as anyone's. It is good business for me to run for mayor. I can make more money on the $10 a week the job pays than I can by doing anything else. I can do it by cutting taxes and gas, light, water and telephone rates. If I am elected, I will do my utmost to accomplish those goals. I can't cut my own taxes and utility bills without doing the same thing for everyone else in Amarillo. If you want those things reduced, vote for me. If not, vote for someone else."

That was all. Ernest was a clever speaker but he was forthright. He never deviated from his platform. One night at a campaign rally a critic charged that he was head-over-heels in debt. Ernest asked Colonel Herring, who was present, if he was the creditor.

"Yes," shouted the colonel, waving his cane vigorously, "and I think it's a damned good loan, too."

When the votes were counted Ernest Thompson, the freckled newsboy, the war hero, the builder, and the proud husband of the Golden Girl, had three-fourths of them. He set out immediately to fulfill his pledge of

54

"taking the penalty out of owning a home." His first official act was a visit to the manager of the gas company. His reception was courteous but cool. The manager was sorry but he was not the man to talk with about rates. That man was Mr. Moody, the president of the parent company, Prairie Oil and Gas Company in Independence, Kansas.

When Ernest sent a telegram requesting an audience with Moody, the reply was that Moody was on a leisurely trip around the world, presently in Cairo, Egypt. Mr. Moody had had ample time during the campaign to decide to make such a trip at that particular time because there was never any doubt about Thompson's election. And he knew enough about the fighting colonel to know that he was a man who would act immediately. But even Mr. Moody's trip had been anticipated by Ernest. In fact, he had his entire program laid out even before he announced for the office. He knew that the gas company was purchasing gas in a field fifty miles away for five cents a thousand cubic feet and selling it in Amarillo for forty-five cents. He also knew that the light-and-power rates were based largely on expenditures for fuel although natural gas was the fuel utilized. And he had familiarized himself with franchise terms for power and telephones. Judge Gaines had taught him thorough planning.

Within a few days the mayor called a press conference at the city hall. He explained his position.

"Gentlemen, my term of office is for only two years," he told the newspapermen. "By the time the president of Prairie gets home that term could expire and my pledge to the voters would be unfulfilled. I am forced to take another course. The city commissioners have approved a plan. We will purchase an old fifty-mile pipeline from the field to an abandoned refinery just outside the city, extend the line into the city, and purchase gas for five cents a thousand cubic feet under a contract we have already made. The waterworks ditching machines will be used to pipe the gas into the city and we will hook up every customer we can reach. We need no bond issue for this since the investment is small and the city needs no franchise. And, incidentally, we will offer gas to the light company for half of the eighteen cents it is now paying and thereby enable that company to reduce its rates, if it cares to do so."

The mayor's proposal met with warm public approval. The line was laid down Third Street where it could tie into both of the mayor's hotels, his building and the power and light company. Within a few weeks he had thirty percent of the commercial and industrial gas business.

As the demand for the cheaper city gas increased, Ernest recommended that the city install a modern, high-pressure gas line to serve the entire city. The city engineer drew up a plan to circle the city with a main line and run arteries from it, like spokes in a wheel, into the heart of the city, providing uniform pressure. He pointed out the advantage of that over the old artificial gas mains in the company's low-pressure system that frequently failed to provide enough gas pressure for cooking and heating during the heavy-demand months. But, he explained, the city would need money and a bond issue would be offered to support the plan. The city could creep into the gas business, as it had already started, but it needed money for a modern and effective system.

The bond campaign was hot, but the mayor never became bitter. The gas company employed every medium available to fight "the invasion of private ownership and the threat of socialism." The city had no money with which to retaliate, but the resourceful Mr. Thompson hit upon another idea. Tom Carnahan, who had been editor of a short-lived Amarillo newspaper and press agent for Ernest's hotels, was given the job as city director of public information. A post-card campaign to reach every utility user in the city was set up. A set of addressed cards was always kept up-to-date. When the mayor had a message he had Carnahan put it into words on the cards and mail them to the citizens. The system proved highly effective and caused the gas company to spend even more than it had anticipated with the newspapers, radio stations and other media.

In the middle of the gas fight the power and light company came to the mayor's terms. He had provided that utility with lower fuel rates, and he had another pretty fair ax. The power franchise was about to expire. That was the first campaign promise to be carried out.

The fight against the gas company had been one without rancor or venom. To Ernest Thompson it was a straight business proposition, like all of the other demands he was making for utility-rate reductions. There was simply no sense in the citizens paying a higher price for a utility than was necessary. The fact of the

57

matter was that he did not want to see the city in the gas business, but he felt if that were the only alternative he would accept it.

His victory actually came before election day. The gas company agreed to reduce its rates to twenty-seven cents a thousand, only two cents over the price the city had asked. In view of that the mayor stopped his campaign by post card and the bond election was lost by a very narrow margin. That, however, amounted to Ernest Thompson's second campaign promise fulfillment. The fact of the matter is that he scared the gas company more than he expected to. He had been willing to settle for some figure between thirty and thirty-five cents all the time.

The next step was the telephone company. In spite of what the Southwestern Bell had seen of Ernest's handling of the gas company, its executives said a rate reduction was impossible and that they were not interested in even discussing the matter.

The city had two approaches to the telephone problem. The first was to determine whether or not the company was making a profit in excess of the legal six and a half percent reasonable return. The second was to refuse renewal of the franchise in the event the profits were excessive. In his typically thorough manner Ernest persuaded the other members of the city commission to join him in a proposal to engage a well-known and highly respected appraisal firm to check the telephone company's property.

The appraisal company did a complete job. It counted every pole, measured every foot of wire, counted the telephone instruments, and checked the company's books completely. Personnel and maintenance costs were considered along with every other possible expense. The report showed the telephone company was exceeding its legal profit by a considerable amount. The company expressed surprise and some doubt in spite of the fact that its own supervisors had accompanied the appraisers and checked their findings, at the mayor's invitation.

The argument was advanced that it would be impossible to reduce Amarillo rates since they were tied to rates in other cities in the Southwestern system and that to reduce one would mean reducing others. The company officials were adamant.

After the final refusal the mayor went to work. He called Carnahan, his public-information man, into a conference and the two decided on their first course. All telephones and switchboards were taken out of both of Ernest's hotels and his building. A messenger service was substituted. Then, with that done, the mayor's post cards appealed to every telephone subscriber in the city to take his telephone off the hook and leave it there until the telephone company came to terms. The citizens responded by the thousands, and the story of the unusual action swept the country. Ernest Thompson, for the second time in months, had become a public hero. But he still employed no violent language. He simply told the company that he was using the only tool at his disposal, public co-operation. Managers from forty-five other cities came to the aid of the Amarillo telephone company and made house-to-house pleas with subscribers to replace their telephones on the hooks, but there were few compliances. Ernest himself suggested that those who had serious illness in their homes keep their telephones in operation.

But with the company still refusing to put rates in line with reasonable profits, the city said it would refuse to renew the telephone franchise. The company took the position that the franchise renewed itself automatically. Former Chief Justice Phillips of the Texas Supreme Court, an old friend of Judge Gaines's and also of Ernest's, was chief counsel of the telephone company and came from Forth Worth to smooth the redhead's determination and to argue the point about the franchise. He remained to lose his own temper at Ernest's stubborn refusal to see his point.

In the closest thing to an explosive mood that he reached during the campaign, Ernest informed Judge Phillips that the telephone company could either reduce its rates or remove its property from the city streets. Failing that, he said, a city crew would be ordered out within three days to chop down every telephone pole located on an easement granted under city franchise, which would expire at that time.

That ended the company's resistance. There was no one in the telephone company who believed Thompson was given to extravagant threats. And the attorneys knew he was probably within his rights. The telephone rates were reduced about fifteen percent. Ernest had suggested twenty percent, but was willing to compromise.

By the time this campaign promise had been taken care of, the mayor and his commissioners realized that the only thing left was for the city to carry out its own rate reductions. The price of water from the city-owned plant was cut by one-third immediately, and tax reductions which eventually amounted to twenty-six percent were made by eliminating waste and employing tighter management.

When he had ended his first term Ernest Thompson was one of the best-known mayors in the country and there wasn't a man within a thousand miles of Amarillo who would think of opposing him. His second term was handed to him on a silver platter. He was, as he always had been, his home town's hero.

In his second term Ernest set about making Amarillo a better place in which to live. He took a 700-acre city dump and converted it into a remarkable park and playground. Water Department ditching machines dug trenches through the acreage twelve feet deep and a thousand feet long. Tons of old cars, tin cans and other junk were ploughed under and covered over by draglines. Then a draw on one end of the park site was dammed up so that the first rain would provide a mammoth lake. The city hired a forester to teach children to plant trees.

Typical depression appeals for dimes were answered with "hole cards" by city policemen. The panhandlers were sent to the park site and given a dime apiece to dig holes for 10,000 trees. Their "hole cards," when punched ten times for digging that many holes, were redeemable at the city hall for a dollar. Then the children of the city were sent in buses to the park site to plant the trees. Each tree bore a metal disc with the name of its sponsoring boy or girl. Twenty years later those children would hold picnics in that park with their own children under their own trees. The park's swimming pool was supplied with pipes that ran through the city incinerator to heat the water enroute. The circulating water from the pool overflowed the park and drained down terraced hills to irrigate the trees constantly. In the middle of the park was a preventorium that would care for sixty tubercular children at once. The park also had an eighteen-hole golf course and six softball diamonds, all lighted. Ernest called the park the Municipal Park; but when he left office, his successors named it, quite appropriately, Thompson Park. The *Dallas News* commented that it took the soul of a poet and the heart of an engineer to convert a dump ground into a thing of beauty and pleasure.

But Ernest Thompson sponsored sixteen more city parks on the basis that they must be built while the city was small and the land was available. Across from the great Municipal Park he built an elaborate playground for Amarillo's Negro citizens. In their section of town he built another park especially for Mexican citizens. When his park commission urged building the parks in the "silk stocking" districts, he discharged the board and appointed a new one that agreed with him that the parks belonged where the most people would use them. A plot four-blocks square in the heart of the town was unused. The neighbors urged the city to build streets and sidewalks and sell the lots to remove the unsightly landscape from the otherwise beautiful city. Ernest and his commissioners took that land and converted it, too, into another tremendous park with winding walkways, a profusion of trees, tennis courts and other recreational attractions. It became known as Ellwood Park, the most popular of all in this city of fine parks.

Before he completed his job Ernest led a movement to top more than a hundred miles of Amarillo's streets with asphalt over caliche rock. He was guest of honor at a meeting in Dallas in May of 1932, and the master of ceremonies dwelt long on his fight against the utility companies and urged that he tell Dallas how he had accomplished the impossible.

"Well," said Ernest with his usual wry grin, "there really wasn't anything to it. Those gentlemen in the utility companies are nice people. They didn't realize they were charging their customers too much. When I called it to their attention, they reduced the rates, and everyone was happy."

There wasn't much left for Ernest to do as mayor when his second term went into the last half of the second year. Amarillo was suffering from the depression, but its people were as prosperous as possible. Their mayor had given the city a million-dollar advertising campaign and people were flocking in from all over the country.

It was in the early afternoon of June 1 that the mayor's telephone rang. It was long distance and Ernest took the call.

"Ernest," came the voice from the other end, "this is Ross Sterling. Can you come to Austin tomorrow?"

"I guess I could, Governor," Ernest replied. "Is it anything important?"

"Certainly it's important," Sterling said. "Do you think I'd be calling the Mayor of Amarillo on a few hours' notice to come down here if it were something trivial?"

Ernest chuckled, assured the governor he would be there, and hung up.

CHAPTER VI

The Governor Calls

Ross Sterling was a good man. He was born on a farm and had worked hard all of his life. His sound judgment and a will to gamble made him a millionaire early in the history of Texas oil when he organized the Humble Oil Company. In 1925 he resigned the Humble presidency and sold his interest after Standard Oil Company of New Jersey took over a majority of the Humble stock.

That year he purchased the *Houston Post* and combined it with the almost defunct little *Houston Dispatch* to form the *Houston Post-Dispatch*. He served with distinction as chairman of the Texas Highway Commission and compiled a record of achievement that catapulted him into the governorship of Texas.

As governor, Sterling was treated as unkindly by the Gods of Fate as any man has ever been treated. By the time he took office the great depression had finally throttled the nation and his state. To add to that burden, the East Texas oil field erupted like a terrible volcano; and to prevent total panic and avoid profligate waste he had to send the Texas National Guard into the field. The head of the Guard was General Jacob Wolters, an old soldier who had served in two wars with distinction, but he was a Texas Company executive. Furthermore, Walter Pyron, one of his colonels, was a production official of the Gulf Oil Company.

This unfortunate set of circumstances, added to Sterling's former Humble connection, mitigated against the governor. Many credulous independent operators and landowners feared big-company domination through the governor. Now, to add to all of Sterling's other problems, the one man of stature on the Railroad Commission had given notice of his resignation. Pat Neff, brilliant former governor and chairman of the Commission which was charged with the regulation of the oil-and-gas industry in the state, had accepted the presidency of Baylor University. There had to be a successor and he had to be a man the people would respect and trust.

The governor was addressing the young man from Amarillo.

"Ernest," he said, "Pat Neff is resigning from the Railroad Commission and I have called you down here to ask you to take the job."

Sterling said that he realized he was asking Thompson to make a great sacrifice, but that the situation called for a man with the courage and the force to serve the state. He spoke of the challenge, as well as the opportunity for service.

"Son," the governor said, "I guess I am asking a lot. This job is no bed of roses. You will be criticized and condemned from all sides. But you are the only man who meets all of the qualifications. Your war record and your dramatic accomplishments as mayor of Amarillo will stand you in good stead when unfair and unscrupulous men vilify you. Fortunately you are neither rich nor an oil man. I think you know the mess we are in. I know you are the one man who can help the most. Will you take the job?"

Ernest thought for a moment. He realized that he could hold the position from June until January without offering for election. But, should his services be required beyond January, he would have to announce and make a state-wide political campaign. He asked the governor if it would help to serve until January.

"That won't be enough, Ernest," the governor said. "I have called you because you are needed until this thing is cleared up. The trouble won't be over by January. I want you especially because you seem to be the only sound man who can win the upcoming election. Your record will get you votes. You will be virtually unassailable, although you probably will be falsely accused of much before you are elected. There will be other men in the race. I don't know who they will be. I do know that if an incompetent or a crook should win the office Texas would be doomed. You must run for election."

Thompson realized that the task he was being asked to perform was a remarkable challenge. He was confident that he could serve well and he was flattered that he should be called upon under the conditions.

"Governor, it will be a privilege to serve the state the way you put it," Thompson said. "I'll do my best."

Sterling appointed Thompson and Neff resigned. The

colonel made arrangements to announce for election to the office in the Democratic primaries that same day, June 4, 1932.

The Texas Railroad Commission became the regulatory body for the oil industry in Texas by a process of evolution. The Commission was originally established to deal with the iniquities that grew up within the railroad industry in the state. The first to recognize and challenge the evils was James Stephen Hogg when he was a young and forceful attorney general. Hogg, the trust-buster, is revered in the state as second only to the immortal Sam Houston as chief executive. As attorney general he called attention to illegal bond promotions, rebates, discriminatory freight rates and profits far in excess of reasonable returns. On the same ballot there was a constitutional amendment that called for the establishment of a commission with duties similar to those of the newly created Interstate Commerce Commission. Both Hogg and the constitutional amendment won overwhelmingly.

As soon as a law was passed by the legislature in 1891 establishing a three-man commission to be appointed by the governor, Hogg persuaded John H. Reagan to give up his seat in the United States Senate to accept the chairmanship. Reagan, who had been the postmaster general of the Confederacy during the Civil War, gave the position dignity and authority. In 1894 when Hogg left the governorship the legislature made the offices elective for six-year terms with one post becoming subject to a vote of the people every two years.

With the coming of the motor age the Commission

took on the task of regulating motor bus and truck transportation, since most of the illegal practices it had been established to curtail had been eliminated. The legislature then added the task of regulating gas utilities and setting rates. Later, the state began to regulate the rapidly expanding oil and gas pipeline systems and that function also fell on the Railroad Commission since both railroads and pipelines were common carriers and hence fell in the same category of regulation.

About 1919 new Texas oil discoveries were popping up in every direction. Never did a state have as many different booms going on at one time. All combined they were nothing like East Texas, but up to that time they were the wildest oil booms ever seen. As far back as Spindletop there had been safety committees within fields, and even as far back as 1899 the state legislature had passed a law to curb oil and gas waste. In 1919 Governor W. P. Hobby signed a bill written by Senator R. L. Carlock of Fort Worth that gave the state more effective control over the conservation of its natural resources. The law was aimed at such rampant booms and disastrous fires as those in Burkburnett, Ranger, Desdemona and West Columbia.

When the legislature passed the law, which still serves as the basis of all conservation measures in Texas, the Railroad Commission was assigned to the task of enforcing it. The Commission was charged with prevention of physical waste but the law emphasized that economic waste was not to be considered.

The first oil-and-gas division-chief was one of Texas' most distinguished lawyers, Dr. George C. Butte. Dr.

Butte took a leave of absence from the University of Texas law school to draw up the regulations for both the gas utilities and the oil-and-gas divisions at the request of Governor Hobby. A prominent international lawyer, Dr. Butte was chief of foreign intelligence for the War Department General Staff in the First World War, dean of the law school at the University of Texas, the man who came closest to winning the governorship of Texas as a Republican, attorney general of Puerto Rico and governor general of the Philippines. His contribution, along with those of John H. Reagan, the first chairman, and Allison Mayfield, put regulation on a sound basis.

After the flush production of 1919 and 1920 that flooded the oil market, the commission had its troubles with Mexia field which became a new center of boom and chaos. There General Jacob Wolters had his first assignment in enforcing martial law in an oil field by order of Governor Pat Neff.

As the years passed Spindletop came back in 1926 to set off an entirely new series of discoveries including Yates, Hendricks, Van and Darst Creek. Van came just a year before East Texas; and even before Dad Joiner's tremendous strike Texas was flooded with an oil potential of millions of barrels. The first state-wide order in 1930 held production to 775,000 barrels daily and brought lawsuits, injunctions, and criticism against the Commission. Even then the state's potential production was in excess of 2,000,000 barrels daily.

That, briefly, was the history of the Commission to which Colonel Thompson had been appointed. The East

Texas discovery presented new problems that came with the same regularity as its new wells. The Commission had taken little action in the field until after it was six months old. Then it was too late to enforce proration, spacing or any of the other rules that Dr. Butte had written with foresight and wisdom.

But East Texas' tidal wave of oil had washed out all reason and co-operation. The legislature had provided no teeth for the enforcement of the Commission's rules. There was nothing that could be done to a violator except to sue him and that was an empty gesture in most instances.

Dr. Butte's rules included one that was to be the exception that proved the rule. They called it Rule 37. It enabled any landowner, however small his tract, to have one well if he could drill it. With the oil sand so shallow, the drilling so easy and the cost so cheap, more than half of the wells in the field were necessary exceptions to the spacing pattern under Rule 37.

Most major companies had lost faith in the area. Their experts had told them there was nothing there because there was no structure. Most of the country had been under lease to majors, or capable independents, until a year or so before the Joiner well came in. All except Sinclair had backed out on advice of the exploration advisers and left a clear field to thousands of small get-rich-quick shoestringers. Oil men were accustomed to co-operating with the Commission up to a certain point, but these boom-born wildcatters had never even heard of oil-field regulations. Even if the Commission had been alert in trying to do something before the field got out of hand it is not likely that the money-mad boomers would have heeded their orders.

When trouble arose and orders started coming out of Austin six months late no one paid the least bit of attention to them. So-called enforcement officers were met with shotguns and pistols and chased off leases. One well was covered with a concrete blockhouse. The governor called one special session after another in an effort to get a law with authority, but the legislature balked and played politics. The people could get no inkling of the importance of the danger to their leading industry because, unfortunately, the press had few trained oil writers who could understand its implications and interpret them to its readers.

Without a market-demand law there was no way of putting a ceiling on field production until someone could define physical waste. There had to be a figure based on some tangible fact to prove waste before the Commission could write an order that would stand up. The consequence was lawsuits, injunctions and physical resistance to every effort to curb wanton drilling and production. The governor, despite the fact that he wanted a workable law and despite the fact that he was accused of playing footsie with the majors, had announced that he would veto any law that authorized the consideration of market demand, the very thing the majors advocated most.

But the situation went from bad to worse. Every day and every new barrel of oil brought new crises in the industry. On August 4, 1931, Governor Alfalfa Bill Murray of Oklahoma ordered the Oklahoma City and Greater Seminole fields closed in by state troops. Within two or three days a group of East Texans appealed to Sterling to shut East Texas down until order could be obtained. On August 12 the legislature did pass a new oil-and-gas-conservation law and it specifically directed that market demand was not to be considered in its enforcement. On August 15 the governor ordered the National Guard into East Texas to shut in and control production until an order could be written in compliance with the new law.

On September 5, the Railroad Commission set allowables at 225 barrels and the field was reopened. That was just about the economic break-even point for the small operators, and they had a difficult time meeting their obligations with such meager returns. A month later a national committee of oil regulatory officers from several states, representatives of both major and independent companies and government officials, urged that the field be cut another 100,000 barrels daily to balance supply with national demand. Output was then reduced to 185 barrels per well a day.

This brought court action designed to prevent the National Guard from enforcing Railroad Commission orders. Thereupon the governor issued his own orders to replace Commission orders. This brought on the famous Constantin case wherein the governor's right to maintain martial law in the absence of riots and insurrection was challenged. E. Constantin and other independent operators financed the suit. Even as the case was in court the price of oil had increased to 85 cents in spite of unbridled drilling activity.

A three-judge federal court agreed with Constantin, and the governor was ordered to remove the troops. The governor kept the troops in the field and delayed the day of their departure while the state appealed the case to the United States Supreme Court. No solution was in sight, so the state resorted to as many dilatory tactics as possible since it was obvious that the use of troops was unconstitutional. Sterling was playing for time and hoping for a trace of sunshine to come through the thick clouds of chaos and confusion.

One of the delaying tactics employed by the governor was to return the Commission to control of the field and to leave the guardsmen there to act as peace officers. The first thing the Commission did upon its return was to issue a new order dropping allowables to seventy-five barrels a day. This was necessitated by the ever-increasing number of wells being drilled.

It was about the time that the Commission was forced to reduce allowables to forty-three barrels a day that Governor Neff heeded the call to Baylor, and Sterling called upon Thompson. All of this Sterling explained to Thompson as a prelude to offering him the position on the Commission. In the face of all of it, however, Thompson accepted and promised to do his best.

The colonel had little chance to do so much as turn a hand in helping Smith and Terrell with East Texas immediately. His first problem was to plan a political campaign which was absolutely necessary to his continuation on the Commission. For that reason alone he could devote little time to his official duties. Neff offered to withhold his resignation until after the election which would have enabled Thompson to serve two years without an election, but Thompson preferred to make an immediate announcement submitting his candidacy to the voters. The former governor was glad to retire to the quiet of the Waco campus and escape the bombardment of criticism and the loud and discordant chorus of demands and counter-demands.

Another serious problem faced by the colonel was the fact that he was not acquainted with the Commission or its responsibilities and felt compelled to learn all he could. The fact that he had several cases pending before the Utilities Division wherein he was the attorney representing cities seeking lower gas rates had given him some experience in that field. Of course, he had recused himself from sitting in hearings in that Division on his suits. But he had to acquaint himself with the Pipeline and the Railroad Divisions in addition to the Oil and Gas Division. Injunctions and lawsuits against the Commission in oil-and-gas matters had been so numerous that he was forced to spend a great deal of time acquainting himself with those details also.

Colonel Thompson's appointment and his candidacy were both received warmly by most of the press. Since the governor had addressed him as "colonel" in the original announcement, the title of mayor slipped into obscurity almost immediately. The newspapers liked the new title because of its elasticity. They could either abbreviate it or spell it out, depending on the head count necessary. More important, however, was that the title seemed to fit the man. He was colorful, crisp, correct and convincing. And he was self-confident, exacting and effectively efficient. His whole record and background spoke for his integrity and devotion to public duty. The colonel's bearing was military and his voice and manner both carried authority. The Texas press seemed well pleased with this new man of the hour.

The oil industry welcomed his appointment officially, but actually paid little attention to it at first. The industry, as a matter of fact, had little regard for the Railroad Commission. It had been behind Sterling's idea to turn oil-and-gas matters over to an appointed board of experts to be known as the Oil and Gas Commission, or the Conservation Commission of Texas, or some other appropriate name. It was fed up with the ineffectual efforts of a three-man board that headed a jambalaya of hodgepodge bureaus. Many considered it a political graveyard which served as a just reward for political retreads. It paid fairly well as political jobs go and it was dignified and required its members to offer for office only once every six years. The Commission had degenerated into that in public opinion since the days of such stalwarts as the great John H. Reagan, Governor Colquitt, and Thompson's old crony of the Judge Gaines days, Allison Mayfield. Mayfield spent twenty-six years on the Commission and, when Thompson was with Judge Gaines, he had spent many evenings talking to the boy about his duties which had to do largely with regulating railroads.

In those days the Commission had a single purpose

and a membership of high caliber. Now the Commission had five times the responsibility and none of the old masters. No one looked upon Thompson as another Reagan.

But the industry leaders threw their weight behind the colonel because he was Sterling's appointee and would probably try to do right even if his grasp of oil-and-gas problems was limited.

In the July primary, the colonel drew three opponents for his position. The most formidable was Gregory Hatcher, a former state treasurer whose name had some political appeal. Another was Olin Culberson, a vigorous man of high morals and determination who also had a name familiar in Texas politics. The third was a political unknown named Ed Murphy.

Texas has two Democratic primaries each even year of the calendar. In the race for a particular office, like that of the Railroad Commission, a candidate for the Democratic nomination must receive a majority. If not, the two high vote-getters are required to hold a run-off primary, a month later, in August. Democratic nomination is the same as election.

The colonel did not make a full-fledged campaign. The people of Texas up to that time had never taken a serious interest in political races except those for Governor, Congress, or sheriff. The other races were mere window dressing and that included the race for the Railroad Commission. The fact is that most voters had little or no conception of the meaning or importance of the Commission.

In this year of 1932 Ross Sterling faced Miriam A. Ferguson again. Mrs. Ferguson was the wife of the former Governor Jim Ferguson who had been impeached in 1917 and denied the right to hold office again in Texas. In 1924 Mrs. Ferguson, running on her husband's slogan of "Two Governors for the price of one" had become the first woman in the United States to hold the governorship of a state. In 1926 she had been defeated. In 1930 she opposed Sterling when he was elected. With the depression in full swing and with East Texas' chaos heaping coals of criticism and abuse upon the governor, the Fergusons decided the time was ripe to avenge their loss of 1930. As it turned out, they guessed right. The good man from Houston would go down in defeat in the second primary by the narrowest of margins. He would go home in January to find that his vast fortune had been scattered by the inevitable forces of economic depression.

But the Ferguson race concerned Colonel Thompson also. His run-off opponent, Hatcher, had attempted to cling to the Ferguson coattails and petticoats, but the Fergusons would have no part of him. Thompson's campaign manager, Carl Calloway, dug up a 1926 news clipping in which Ferguson had called Hatcher one of the worst enemies he ever had. Hatcher had been appointed treasurer by Ferguson and had then broken with him. The backfiring of this Hatcher shell did much for Thompson.

Hatcher's greatest mistake, however, was his attack on Thompson's title of colonel. "The appointed colonel"; "The colonel of whatnot"; and "The colonel in such a way as to cast a slur on the military title." Those aspersions were too much for the colonel's old buddies in the 90th Division and the American Legion over the state. They rose up in arms to his defense and carried on a campaign that swamped Hatcher beneath an avalanche of votes in the second primary. Hatcher's charges of the colonel's collusion with the big oil companies had some effect in East Texas. But even that part of the state was swayed the night that the colonel made his only major campaign address of the run-off at Tyler. He reminded the vast audience that as Mayor of Amarillo he had carried out his campaign promises and had opposed the big utilities until they were willing to consider the public interest. His only accusation against Hatcher came that night, too, when in reply to Hatcher's charge that the big companies were behind Thompson, the colonel denied the charge. He said it was probable that the utilities, most of whom he had embarrassed in Amarillo and since then, were out to chastise him by helping elect Hatcher.

The colonel also had the help of the other two candidates in the run-off. Both had been approached by Hatcher for their endorsements and both had, instead, thrown their weight behind Thompson. This was a profit the colonel reaped for his dignified first primary campaign wherein he mentioned no opponent by name except in a complimentary manner.

His campaign method was to answer any damaging charges and to say that he intended to try to do the same thing for the state that he had done for his home town. He was forthright in his discussions about the oil problem. One of his greatest embarrassments was the fact that while he was campaigning, the commission had been forced to cut the per well allowables in East Texas to forty-three barrels a day. This action incensed the East Texans and Hatcher made the most of it. Still, when it was all over, Thompson had again shown himself to be equal to the task. It was the year of Franklin D. Roosevelt's election and the year of Sterling's defeat. The turbulence of the economic storm had wrought great political changes.

In the weeks immediately after his election, Thompson spent much of his time attending to the other duties of the Commission while Terrell and Smith tried to bring the East Texas picture into focus. Their efforts were uniformly unsuccessful. Their orders were subjected to injunction suits and the oil operators continued to produce as if there were no allowables.

East Texas became more and more confused. On December 12 the United States Supreme Court ruled against the state in the Constantin case. The ruling was as the governor and all concerned knew it would be. The troops were now without authority to remain in the field.

Governor Sterling, who seems to have been elected for his one term as a man of destiny, had prevented almost single-handedly the complete collapse of the oil industry. He had sacrificed his political career and lost his personal fortune so he was to return home with only his record. That record was a greater accomplishment than most public officers could claim in a dozen political careers.

The Commission knew that one of its members must

take up temporary headquarters in the field. Smith and Terrell were too old for such a strenuous task. They requested Thompson to take on the responsibility.

Thompson was as flattered by the confidence of his colleagues as he had been by that of the governor. He looked upon it as an opportunity to do something about the challenge he had promised Sterling he would accept.

It was only a few days later that Ernest O. Thompson presented himself in General Jake Wolters' tent and announced that he was there to take over.

CHAPTER VII

Proration Hill

Proration Hill was no picnic ground. Jake Wolters'
canvas-covered chair under the pyramidal army tent
could not be called comfortable in December of 1932.
Not only was East Texas growing wilder and more cor-
rupt each day, but the national depression was at its
very darkest point.

Ernest Thompson had taken over the hill and he was
aware that he had a job on his hands. He thought of the
peace and quiet of Amarillo and how he could do no
wrong there. Kilgore and its turbulent surroundings
would be precisely the opposite. There would be no
peace. Nothing he could do for the next year or so could
possibly be right in the eyes of East Texans.

There were many smart oil men in East Texas. They
knew the business and they told each other and the
colonel what should be done. The trouble was that no
two of them had the same plan. Most of the oil operators
and companies were honest in their efforts. But they
lacked the spirit of sacrifice. They applauded regulations
when applied to others and objected when the same
regulations applied to them. This bonanza was too good.
The majors were trying to tell everyone what to do but

82

they fumbled the ball and the little independents had brought the field in and leased up most of the acreage. There was a suspicion that the big companies were trying artificially to curtail production so they could force out the little men. Ernest Thompson had not dismissed that possibility completely from his own mind. Yet he knew that cutthroat competition was not helping anyone.

But Ernest Thompson's mission in East Texas had nothing to do with all of that. His mission was to prevent physical waste. At his behest the Texas legislature in November of 1932 had passed a market-demand law. That was the second intelligent piece of legislation passed to combat physical waste. The first had elevated the Commission from the mission of an oil-field safety committee charged with the prevention of oil-field fires and blowouts to one with the power to prorate production, to space wells, and to issue or deny drilling permits. But even that law had no teeth. There was nothing the Commission could do if an oil man decided he would go contrary to the Commission's orders. Up to the time of East Texas, of course, most of the orders had actually been agreements arrived at by a central committee of oil companies and independent operators.

Now things were different. The Railroad Commission actually had the authority to prevent physical waste. No one in the oil business was accustomed to such state authority and most people in the business resented it. But Ernest Thompson saw the problem from the viewpoint of a citizen who didn't want the state's natural resources squandered simply to keep companies prosperous and make men rich. He had no axes to grind and he had no favors to hand out. And best of all he had no obligations to pay or ties that bound him. Whereas oil men of all breeds had their own bias and prejudice and interests, and the landowners and businessmen in oil towns had their self-interests to serve, Ernest Thompson had none of this. Even the older politicians, like Terrell and Smith, and Ross Sterling had political obligations. He hadn't asked Sterling for this job; Sterling had come to him. No one had put up money for his campaign. Some oil men had backed him on their own, but others had backed his opponents. Ernest Thompson was probably the only man in Texas, or maybe in the country, who could do this job without the fear of stepping on some friend's toes, crossing a board of directors somewhere, irritating a boss, or acting without some kind of personal self-interest. He had no oil interest or royalty or stock. He didn't own land that might someday become oil land. Naturally, he didn't know as much about production and conservation as men like Jake Wolters; or Underwood Nazro, the Gulf man; or J. Edgar Pew, the Sun Oil man; or Bill Farish of Standard of Jersey; or any of the others whose counsel he would have. He would seek their advice because they knew the industry. But he didn't have to take it. His one obligation, as it kept coming back to him, was to the people of Texas. This great natural resource was theirs; it was valuable and irreplaceable. It was like water in a well; it would play out in time. And if the well were not operated with a thought toward reservoir pressure, it would play out before all of the water had been drawn.

EAST TEXAS OIL FIELD

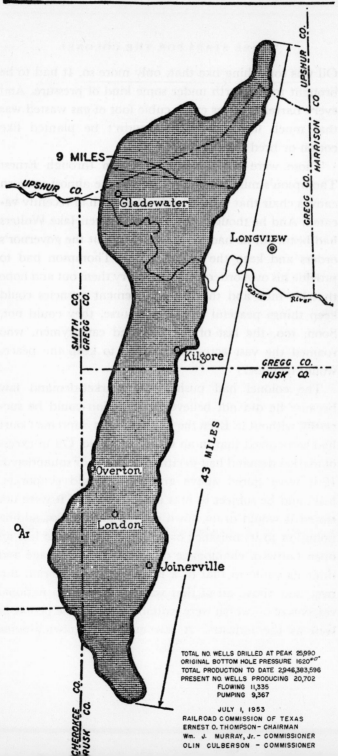

9 MILES

UPSHUR CO.

Gladewater

LONGVIEW

Sabine River

Kilgore

GREGG CO.
RUSK CO.

SMITH CO.
GREGG CO.

UPSHUR CO.

GREGG CO.
HARRISON CO.

43 MILES

Overton

London

Ar

Joinerville

CHEROKEE CO.
RUSK CO.

TOTAL NO. WELLS DRILLED AT PEAK 25,990
ORIGINAL BOTTOM HOLE PRESSURE 1620#"0"
TOTAL PRODUCTION TO DATE 2,946,383,596
PRESENT NO. WELLS PRODUCING 20,702
FLOWING 11,335
PUMPING 9,367

JULY 1, 1953
RAILROAD COMMISSION OF TEXAS
ERNEST O. THOMPSON - CHAIRMAN
Wm. J. MURRAY, Jr. - COMMISSIONER
OLIN CULBERSON - COMMISSIONER

Oil was something like that, only more so. It had to be brought to the earth under some kind of pressure. And every barrel of oil or every cubic foot of gas wasted was that much lost forever. It couldn't be planted like cotton or bred like cattle.

Those were the thoughts that ran through Ernest Thompson's mind as he sat there in the almost unworn canvas chair that General Jake Wolters had recently vacated. And he thought how fortunate even Jake Wolters had been. All he had to do was carry out the governor's orders and keep the peace. Ernest Thompson had to provide his own orders and then carry them out and hope that his men and the law enforcement agencies could keep things peaceful which, of course, they could not. Soon, too, the last of the mounted cavalrymen, who roamed the vast acres of the field to keep the peace, would be gone.

The colonel had pushed the market-demand law because he did not believe conservation could be successful without it. Even the United States Supreme Court had recognized that in an Oklahoma case. Oil in excess of market demand had to either be stored or squandered. If it were stored above ground it would evaporate, leak, and be subject to fires and weather. If it were not stored it would drain down ditches and creeks, adding pollution to its nuisance or it would deteriorate like an open bottle of champagne or carbonated beverage and limit its value to that of a road topping material. But over and above all of that was the danger to national reserves of oil which were valuable to all of the people as well as the industry. A few cut-throat-get-rich-quick pirates could not be permitted to destroy what had already become the most important natural resource in the world. Some would shout about price-fixing and monopoly. Others would cry cutthroat competition and chaos, and Ernest Thompson would have to take it. He was resigned to that fate.

But he knew that he would have trouble with some big oil companies. They would not only try to help him, they would try to lead him. They would think he should be impressed by their importance. The mistake they were making in their man was monumental. Pretty soon big-company officials would be saying that Ernest Thompson wouldn't stand hitched. And he wouldn't. He would go along with anyone he thought was right, but he would turn his back on anyone who changed course to the right or the left of the good road.

When the colonel first went to East Texas in December to relieve Jake Wolters he considered his mission there one of short duration. He had an idea that if he put a system of some kind into operation, his employees could carry on the work. He was impressed with E. O. Buck, a young engineer who had gone to work early as chief engineer in the field. Buck had recently come up with a formula for setting allowables that answered some of the criticism heaped on the Commission's per well basis. Buck's formula took into consideration both acreage and bottom hole pressure. The order for December 11 in East Texas had included the formula but was certain to be stricken down by the courts as all of the others had been. That order provided an average of thirty-seven barrels per well for the 9018 oil wells in the field. The engineers said the field could produce 450,000 barrels without danger to the reservoir, and the national committee had asked that 100,000 barrels be reduced from that figure in the interest of market demand. That was why, whatever formula was used, the total legal production for the field could not exceed 350,000 barrels daily.

Thompson could see the fallacy of such orders and he was not antagonistic toward the courts which threw them out. There had to be more evidence than the number of producing wells divided by a top-field allowable. He worked out a plan whereby he could know every well in the field. It was simply a card index that showed the well number, the lease, the acreage, the operator, date of completion, production depth and outlet or market for the oil. The colonel then asked Buck to get him a good map of the field showing every well, the productive extent and the estimated future extent of the field. He wanted to know about the reservoir from both an engineering and geological standpoint.

Buck and the other engineers prepared a grid map of the entire East Texas field. The map was crossed with north-south and east-west lines a mile apart. The colonel borrowed on his military training to work out the plan with his engineers. Wells located at or near the corners of each grid and those in the center of each square were spotted. These were designated as key wells which would be tested to determine bottom hole pressure and other reservoir conditions. There were 323 key wells marked on the huge map.

A committee of East Texans headed by Carl Estes, a

prominent newspaperman, had suggested closing the field for a month to obtain data to support a valid field order. Thompson explained that to Buck and asked his advice. Buck said that he believed a shutdown could help the engineers determine whether or not the field had a water drive and important facts about bottom hole pressures. But he advised against closing down for more than two weeks. That was about the time it would take a court to act on an injunction. If the enjoiners knew that the shutdown would be over by the time they could get action, they would probably not act.

December 17 was a significant day. For the first time in thirty years a heavy snow fell all over East Texas. The horse-borne troopers, who were scheduled to leave the field on December 21, a handful of Commission investigators, and a company of Texas Rangers went over the field with Thompson and Buck, closing in wells. Everything wasn't rosy. Several operators balked and refused, chasing Commission investigators off leases with guns and knives. By the close of the day on December 19, however, every well in the field except six had been closed in. Those six were fenced in and the operators threatened investigators with violence if they entered the enclosures.

It was early on the morning of December 20 that the colonel got a long-distance call from his mother in Amarillo. She informed him that his father was critically ill and that he should come home as soon as possible. As she talked, L. O. Thompson insisted on talking with his son.

"Ernest," he said with a feeble but determined voice, "I see in the *Dallas News* that you have all except six wells closed in. Don't leave there until every well is down. If you do, they will all be flowing before you can get back. Close them yourself and then come home."

Ernest Thompson promised and put the telephone down. He knew his father's advice was sound. He called the Ranger captain and asked for enough men to shut down the fenced-in wells. Thompson and the captain, following the big map, went to each of the wells and called the operators' bluff with an offer to shoot it out. The threat worked and each well was closed down with a Ranger left on guard to keep it closed.

Back in the little tent on Proration Hill before noon, Thompson had another call from Amarillo. L. O. Thompson had died at 10 o'clock. The sadness of the news was softened for the colonel by the satisfaction of having carried out his father's last order.

New Year's Day brought the end of one of the most remarkable years in petroleum history. East Texas had produced more oil that year than the fabulous Spindle-top field had produced in its thirty-one years, including two tremendous world-shaking booms. In 1932 almost sixty percent of all of the oil wells completed in the United States were drilled in East Texas. The shutdown that had lasted two weeks had taken almost five million barrels of excess oil off the glutted market.

On January 1 the field was opened again on a twenty-eight-barrel per well allowable basis. This was a temporary move until the bottom hole pressure information could be studied and co-ordinated. Ten days later, using Buck's formula, and the accumulated data of the shutdown, the allowables were increased to thirty-one barrels per well. During this period Thompson had returned to Austin to handle matters that had piled up on his desk there. He was leaving utility, pipeline and railroad hearings to their respective department heads and the other commissioners. Olin Culberson, the first primary opponent, who had frequently asked people to vote for Thompson if they could not vote for him, had been appointed chief of the gas-utilities division where he would render outstanding service that would later lead to his elevation to the Commission itself.

About the middle of January the colonel was forced to return to the field to take up a station that would require most of his personal attention for the next two or three years. The last of the National Guardsmen had left the field a few days before Christmas and additional Railroad Commission investigators had replaced them. Thompson's return to the field had been necessitated by a plea on the part of the East Texas Producers and Royalty Owners Association who had asked that otherwise some law enforcement agency relieve the Commission of its duties. Thompson said the responsibility belonged to the Commission and that the Commission would handle it. Matters were getting worse all of the time. The hot oil runners, who had come into being with the first proration orders after the governor's field shutdown in August of 1931, were growing bolder. They were tapping lines to steal oil, and using every conceivable trick to circumvent regulations. They were aware that there was little penalty for their crime under the law, even when they were caught.

As the Ferguson administration started there was a

new cry for an oil-and-gas-conservation commission. It was proposed that the governor appoint three men to such a commission, each with a salary of $6000 a year. This was, of course, a political move by Ferguson followers who saw the important implications in controlling so vast a resource. The bill squeezed through the Texas lower house and was on the floor of the Senate when Thompson made his plea.

"Gentlemen," he told the senators who were behind the bill, "I am new on this Commission. Please give me time to hang up my hat before you take my job away from me. I believe we are doing as much as any other commission could do, particularly an appointed one."

His plea was successful. The bill did not reach the Senate floor. Things in the field continued, however, to get worse. Railroad Commission employees were being chased off leases at gun point. Pipelines were being dynamited. A blockhouse was built around a well near Gladewater. Some operators cut down the ladders to their storage tanks to prevent investigators from gauging their oil. One of the Commission's most welcome aids, although illegal, was a self-appointed vigilante committee composed of six men and three women that roamed the field seeking out hot-oil producers and shutting in their wells.

One day Thompson noticed that he was being trailed by a big-hatted, high-booted Ferguson Ranger. The officer refused to answer his questions, and Thompson went to Austin to see the governor. He met Jim Ferguson in the governor's outer office and protested the shadowing.

"Let's go in and see Mama about it, Ernest," the former governor said and they proceeded to Governor Ma Ferguson's office. There Jim winked at his wife and said: "Mama, Ernest says our Rangers are trailing him in East Texas and that he doesn't like it."

Mrs. Ferguson smiled and explained that she had received reports that his life was in danger and that she knew he would refuse protection, so she had put two Rangers in the field to see that nothing happened to him.

"Governor, I am most grateful," Thompson replied. "As a matter of fact, I need more Rangers to help our men enforce the law."

Mrs. Ferguson said that he would have them and that they would report to him for duty as soon as he returned to the field.

In March of 1933 the Commission again closed down the East Texas field for two weeks to take bottom hole pressures and check the findings with the first shutdown. Operators had challenged the finding of the first shutdown, saying Commission engineers had no idea what they were doing. The pressures were dropping rapidly in the field, indicating a dangerous loss of reservoir energy due to the inordinate number of holes drilled. During the second Thompson shutdown the pressure built up nine pounds. It gave the Commission some physical facts to take into the courts.

During the period, however, many operators were unable to reconcile the fact that a flowing well which required no pumping to lift the oil, was allowed to produce only 31 barrels a day with the fact that a marginal, or pumping well, was allowed to produce 40 barrels of oil a day. The inconsistency of such a proration order also puzzled the court. It seemed logical that a good oil well, under any kind of order, should be permitted at least as much production as a poor well. The fact was that the state marginal well law, passed before the discovery of East Texas, provided that an oil well drilled to a depth of 3500 feet should be permitted to make a minimum of 40 barrels of oil a day if it could do so. On the other hand, there was no limit to how much or how little a well which required no artificial lift, like pumping equipment, could make. On this point the court again threw out the Commission's proration order for East Texas pending clarification.

One day in April the Commission was ordered to appear in person before Judge Randolph Bryant in Sherman. Thompson had gone to the University with the judge so the other Commissioners elected him to make the appearance for all three. The order said the Commission should appear before the court at exactly 10 A.M. to answer a contempt citation. At that exact moment Thompson walked into the courtroom. An insurance case was being heard by Judge Bryant. Thompson ignored the lawyers on both sides and stood, hat in hand, directly in front of Judge Bryant's bench.

After a moment the judge rapped his gavel and asked the colonel what he wanted there.

"Your honor, I represent the Texas Railroad Commission and we have an order signed by this court directing the Commission to appear here at exactly 10 o'clock this morning. It is exactly 10 o'clock now," Thompson replied without a smile.

"Well, Colonel Thompson, would you like to take the matter up in open court or in *chambers?*" Judge Bryant asked with a heavy emphasis on the last word of the question.

"Whatever your honor pleases," replied the stone-faced colonel.

The judge, with a flourish, recessed the court and asked Thompson to follow him to his chambers. After being certain the door was closed, Judge Bryant turned to Thompson and shook his finger vigorously.

"Damn it, Ernest, why didn't you answer that you wanted this taken up in chambers. You knew why I asked the question."

Thompson laughed and his old college classmate looked serious. "Listen, man, if you do something like that to me again I'll put you so far back in that jail they will have to feed you with a slingshot," Bryant said, and then added, "But I'll get in there with you."

Judge Bryant informed Thompson that some men from East Texas had complained against his latest order. Their complaint was that the order was materially the same as the one the court had previously nullified. Judge Bryant called the complainants in to the chambers to present their case. The judge invited Thompson to sit in a chair on his side of the desk while the complaints were heard. When everything was said on both sides Bryant turned to Thompson and said, "Ernest, I don't see anything to all of this. Let's go home to lunch."

That was Judge Bryant's way of showing his respect for Thompson and it had a salutary effect on the colonel's critics. But Bryant did warn Thompson at lunch to issue an order the court could uphold. He said that Judges West and Hutcheson were getting a little weary of hearing the same complaints against the almost identical orders week after week. In 1932 the Commission issued nineteen orders and each one of them was killed by the court.

When the field was reopened after the March shutdown the Commission decided to take drastic action. An order was issued permitting the flowing wells better allowables than the marginal wells. The field allowable, when flush wells were adjusted in proportion to marginal wells, came to almost 775,000 barrels of oil a day. The order was issued on April 22.

But even this order led the Commission into court. The large lease owners demanded that the allowables be based entirely on acreage. Thompson's answer was that some of the major companies had 5000-acre leases whereas some small independents had leases of one or two acres.

"How can there be any fair proportion between 5000 acres and one acre?" he asked.

Another contention was that an acre-foot basis would be fair. An acre-foot is arrived at by measuring the thickness of producing sand and multiplying by the acreage in the lease concerned. One acre-foot is a foot thick and an acre square. Thompson said the thickness of the sand and the area it spread over could not be a true index of potential production. In the second place it would result

in such small relative production for the little lease-
holders that an order written on such a basis would
amount to confiscation of the small operator's property.
There were no suggestions or solutions offered by any
operator, large or small, that would not have benefited
the party offering it.

When all of the arguments were through, the court
handed down its decision upholding the order of April
22, 1933. That was the first valid order issued since East
Texas was discovered. At least, it was the first order upheld in federal court. Five times in less than two weeks
that order was attacked in court and each time the
judges upheld it. Thompson was not happy with the
situation since the engineers for both the oil companies
and the Commission had warned of dangerous pressure
losses in the reservoir if the production exceeded 450,000
barrels a day.

The order did two important things. It gave the Commission a legal standing at last and it almost ruined the
hot-oil operators. Immediately the price of oil fell from
seventy-five cents a barrel to ten cents again and there
was little market for hot oil. Hundreds of thieves and oil
racketeers vanished from the field. Hundreds, but not
all of them. The legitimate operators suffered even more
since their tripled allowables had resulted in a reduction
in price to one-seventh. But the Commission could not
and did not consider price. Some major oil purchasers
and a few large independents refused to pay less than
twenty-five cents a barrel. Others paid royalty to landowners on a twenty-five-cent basis in spite of the fact
that they sold their oil for ten cents.

The April 22 order was issued on the basis of a new method of potentials. Wells were permitted to flow open for two hours to determine their potentiality. It was found that the field could produce more than one hundred million barrels of oil a day. The new order was issued on the basis of fifteen percent of one hour's potential production. The court said the order was based on actual tests instead of on mere speculation. But still operators with wells capable of producing 15,000 barrels a day objected to being cut to fifty or one hundred barrels a day, particularly when wells in other fields were being permitted to produce as much as 2000 barrels daily. The fight had just started. The Commission was at a loss. The fact is that figures were still staring them in the face. East Texas was actually producing more oil than the first allowable set for the whole state three years before.

By the end of May, pressure in East Texas had dropped to 1200 pounds. The field opened with a reservoir pressure of 1600 pounds. The engineers told Ernest Thompson that the critical reservoir pressure was 750 pounds. When the pressure dropped below that point it would be almost impossible to withdraw the inert oil from the sand, and whatever was left at that point probably would remain unrecovered.

Over the next few weeks the allowables were gradually reduced. Each order was attacked, but each time the court upheld the Commission. As the restrictions increased, the hot-oil operations increased. It was a vicious cycle of events. The Commission still had no effective weapon with which to stop hot oil. Finally, at Thompson's urgent request, the legislature passed an important law in September of 1933. Under the new law the production of oil in violation of Commission orders became a felony. This put teeth into enforcement for the first time.

The colonel breathed a little easier. The Rangers could make arrests, with a chance for criminal convictions. His agents could enforce the law. But even as these things were coming about, the national economy had worsened. Later that month the petroleum code of the National Industrial Recovery Act went into effect and federal agents came into East Texas to aid in enforcement.

Shortly before the NIRA code went into effect Thompson had set up a system for approving legally produced oil. He had arranged to give a bill-of-health certificate to every barrel of oil produced under Commission rules. This approval, later to become known as a tender, had to accompany legal oil at all times.

A number of oil shippers sought to evade the law by billing the product out of the state. Thompson refused to let the oil cars move. More than twenty railroad lawyers swooped down on Proration Hill as a result to demand that the cars be allowed to move. Otherwise, they said, their clients would be in violation of Interstate Commerce Commission regulations. The colonel refused to be overwhelmed and the railroads threatened to move the oil over his orders.

Thompson sent an urgent telegram to President Roosevelt stating the problem and suggesting a proclamation banning hot oil from interstate commerce. The next day the President issued an executive order exactly as Thompson had requested it.

Between September and November, with the federal officers on hand to help, allowables were cut back. The basis for this action was the rapidly declining pressure. Gas caps were forming in isolated wells and others were making salt water for the first time. The fallacy of the April 22 order was now apparent. The results convinced even the most violent critics that the engineers were right.

The colonel of Proration Hill was learning his lessons the hard way. His facile mind quickly grasped the points put forward by the petroleum engineers and geologists. He learned to see all sides of every question involving conservation. His judgment was good, and it was fair because he had no obligations and granted no favors.

Still the great laboratory that was East Texas was difficult to control. The oil demand had declined seriously with the depression, at the same time that the greatest source of supply had been uncovered in the form of the Black Giant of East Texas.

Chances are that the Railroad Commission and the state legislature would have worked out all of their problems in time. But the federal officials who showed up in the field in September to act in accordance with the petroleum code of the National Industrial Recovery Act were received with open arms by Ernest Thompson and the other members of the Commission.

CHAPTER VIII

The Colonel and Mr. Ickes

The Blue Eagle came screaming out of the stratosphere of Washington to descend on the derrick tops of East Texas in early September 1933. Immediately its influence began to dispel the clouds of confusion and chaos that had hung over the field for more than two years.

The men on Proration Hill in Kilgore, now occupying a permanent building instead of the little pyramidal tent, welcomed the agents of the National Recovery Administration. Since the day the mounted troopers left the field there had been nothing but trouble. The citizens of East Texas, headed by Carl Estes, had urged some type of enforcement agency. Ernest Thompson had succeeded in getting Rangers, but they could enforce only the peace. They had not and would not assume the responsibility of enforcing Railroad Commission rules and regulations, especially when the federal court consistently threw most of the orders out.

Ernest Thompson had complained that the Commission had been thrown out of court 212 times before it got a valid order and that he himself had been enjoined seven times one day between the capitol building and the Driskill Hotel in Austin where a statewide hearing was scheduled.

But the NRA men came vested with the authority to bottle up illegally produced oil in Texas. You could produce it, you could sell it in Texas, but you couldn't get it beyond the state borders. More than 150,000 barrels of hot oil were being produced and sold daily when they arrived.

Colonel Thompson was glad to see an old friend in charge of the NRA crew of fifty federal investigators. He was Charles I. Francis, a brilliant attorney who had gone through the University of Texas with Thompson. They had been the heads of the two rival ribbon societies on the campus, each composed of fraternity leaders. In Europe they had met when Ernest was with Judge Gaines and Charley was pedaling his way across the continent on a bicycle. They had been in the army together. And now they were in the maelstrom of East Texas together. Charles I. Francis was there to enforce Section 9c of the NIRA which was described as a "code of fair competition for the petroleum industry." He was there by authority of Harold L. Ickes who was Secretary of the Interior, but also held the title of head of the Petroleum Administration Board.

There was only one aspect of this business that Ernest Thompson did not like. He was an implacable foe of federal control. He was born under the star of states' rights and had had it ground into him by a cowboy father and the old Confederate officer, Reuben R. Gaines. But he looked upon the NIRA as an act of emergency to bring prosperity back to a country which was almost hopelessly sunk in depression. The year 1933, for instance, had been a dreary one for oil. Thanks to Sterling's troops, oil had been up to seventy-five cents a barrel in January. Due to the Commission's "valid" order of April 22, with its excessive allowables, prices had again dropped to ten cents. With a gradual reduction in allowables, the price had climbed back to seventy-five cents by early July. But on August 1, with ever-increasing production elsewhere, such as in the mighty Conroe field in South Texas, oil had again dropped to fifty cents. Thirty days after Charles I. Francis and his men took over control of interstate and foreign oil shipments the price would hit the $1 mark Governor Murray had demanded before he would reopen Greater Seminole and Oklahoma City.

The threat of federal control that lurked in the NIRA establishment was real. The code went so far as to suspend all antitrust laws. It was set up to fix prices and absolutely control production by states, fields and even wells, although it had not progressed that far. With men like Charley Francis on the job, the colonel was certain it would not attempt to supersede the authority of the state.

The fabulous bonanza of oil had always attracted the government in Washington. The Republicans, with their ideas of a strong centralized government, probably made the first effective attempt to control the industry in 1924. President Coolidge had established a Federal Conservation Board composed of four cabinet members, including Herbert Hoover. The Board was advised by seven American Petroleum Institute men headed by Amos L. Beaty, one of the pioneers of Spindletop's first great boom, who had become president of The Texas Company. The independents had no use for the Board and referred to it derisively as "The Four Wise Men." The board never had much success, in spite of the valiant efforts of good men of the industry.

Many major oil company men who were members of the American Petroleum Institute actually favored federal control of some kind. They believed that the various states had failed to prevent alarming waste in the capture of oil and that uniformity in production practices was necessary. The independents, on the other hand, had fought vigorously against all controls, even those by the states, on the premise that most curbs enabled major companies to gain control of oil property through proration, spacing and price-fixing. They feared a return of the old Standard Oil type of monopoly which was destroyed by the antitrust laws in 1911. There were good arguments on both sides.

In 1929, only a few months before the great Wall Street market crash, President Hoover called a congress of oil-state governors into session at the Broadmoor Hotel in Colorado Springs and threatened them with federal control if something were not done to curb what he called overproduction. The independents took exception to Hoover's plea because it offered no plan to reduce what they believed were excessive imports. On the second day of the meeting the independents, led by Wirt Franklin of Ardmore, Oklahoma, walked out on the President and went over to the Antlers Hotel where they formed a rip-roaring and highly effective group of their own in opposition to the American Petroleum Institute. They called it the Independent Petroleum Association of America, pledged to stop excessive imports of foreign oil. Soon the new organization set forth on a vigorous program. Two years later they succeeded in persuading Congress to pass excise taxes of twenty-one cents a barrel on imported crude oil and two-and-a-half cents a gallon on foreign gasoline, mostly from Venezuela.

By 1931, with oil wells sprouting alongside of every yellow pine in East Texas, with the nation already confronted with overproduction, the governors of Texas, New Mexico, Kansas and Oklahoma met in Fort Worth to discuss the possibilities of a federal law to permit the oil states to form a compact that would have the authority to enforce uniform conservation laws. At that time none of the states had adequate oil-and-gas laws. E. W. Marland, a giant independent in his own right, and a member of Congress, was the father of the idea. The law was presented to Congress but failed to stir up much interest. All of that was prior to Ernest Thompson's appearance on the oil scene.

In December of 1932, only two days before he went into East Texas to take over, Colonel Thompson made his first blast against federal controls. Hoover was still President, and Secretary of the Interior Wilbur had let it slip that if he had his way every oil well in the United States would be shut down and Americans would use up all of the foreign oil they could consume until it ran out. Secretary Wilbur had the idea that in that way America would be left with the last of this great natural resource available on the face of the earth.

In his argument against federal controls in Fort Worth on December 9, 1932, Colonel Thompson said it would be just as ridiculous to think of controlling cotton or potatoes from Washington as it was to think of controlling oil or gas. He disagreed with the Marland plan of interstate oil compact as one which would "put the noose of federal control around our necks." He warned that the plan meant that a "great monopolistic agency in New York would whisper over private wires down in Washington and tell us what we could do here in Texas. Congress, not being interested in oil since there are only seven or eight important oil-producing states, would pass one law after another until we would be getting our rules and regulations for every well in Texas from some political appointee in Washington."

The irony of the colonel's speech lay in the fact that before another year passed his own party would be in office and have oil, gas, potatoes and cotton under federal control.

Within three months President Roosevelt called a conference of oil-state governors in Washington. There the division between the independents and the majors burst into open warfare again much as it had at the Broadmoor Hotel four years earlier. The independents claimed that Secretary Ickes was playing footsie with the majors. This time Wirt Franklin, the hero of the Independents, was called a tool of the big companies. The Independent Petroleum Association of America was branded with the same iron. Again the independents took a walk and this time they formed what they called the Independent Petroleum Association Opposed to Monopoly. Ickes found himself on the side of the majors and the IPAA. Texans, including Ernest Thompson, hewed to the pure independent line. The battle was on and its culmination was the Petroleum Code under the NRA. At that meeting the Texans, all loyal to Roosevelt and the party, found that the Secretary of the Interior was a little more than they could stomach.

Numerous hearings were held on the oil code in Washington and Colonel Thompson was rarely overlooked as a witness. At one of the very first he suggested that the Bureau of Mines furnish state regulatory bodies with information about consumer demand, imports and withdrawal from storage. That would be a most effective way, he said, for regulatory bodies to determine market demand. At the same hearing the colonel said that it was disheartening to him to see foreign imports increase by the amount of the reduction in East Texas allowables.

There was never any mutual affection between Ernest Thompson and Harold Ickes. Few Texas oil men had much regard for Ickes. Even Attorney General James V. Allred, whose devotion to the New Deal was above question, frequently and effectively clashed with the Interior Secretary. Ernest usually led the way to enlightenment. He often reminded the press in Texas that Texas had agreed to no code and that Ickes did not control production in Texas.

Ickes' high-handed ignorance in oil-industry problems was often a cause for bitterness. On one occasion a Harrison and Abercrombie well at Conroe had gone wild in one of the most disastrous blowouts in Texas history. Every effort was being made to close it in and prevent its being ignited. A great moat was built around the well to catch the oil. Numerous attempts were made to get it under control, but all had failed. Railroad Commission and company field engineers from both independent and major companies were trying everything known to petroleum science and practical experience. In the midst of the struggle Colonel Thompson received a telegram from Ickes ordering that this wild well be shut in.

Several hours later Thompson, fresh from the scene of the wild well, called Ickes on the telephone to report.

"Mr. Secretary," he said, "I have read your telegram to the wild well in Conroe and it is still blowing. Do you have any other further suggestions?" The Secretary hung up the phone.

On another occasion Ickes ordered that the newly discovered Cayuga field be limited to seven wells in 1934. The order was, of course, preposterous since there was only one well at that time and hundreds of leases around the discovery. Thompson merely asked the Secretary which seven wells he thought should be drilled and then reminded him that the Texas Railroad Commission would make that or any other decisions on matters pertaining to the regulation of the oil-and-gas industry within the state of Texas. Thompson suspected Ickes of promoting compulsory unitization of the field. He believed that would mitigate against the independents in favor of the majors.

By 1934 Ickes and the administration began to get a hint that the NRA would not last. Ickes immediately set out to have a law passed that would replace the Petroleum Code. The bill, sponsored by Senator Elmer Thomas and Representative Wesley Disney, both of Oklahoma, would have made Ickes permanent oil administrator. "The only recourse," Thompson told the investigating committee, "would be in the faraway District of Columbia Court of Appeals. Texans will not willingly accept such a law."

The bill also provided that oil from a new source could not enter commerce until a scientific development plan had been worked out by the administrator. Then Thompson cited the Cayuga incident. Under Thompson's guidance the entire Texas delegation in Washington, including Vice-President John Garner, Senator Tom Connally and Speaker Sam Rayburn, and Texas Congressmen, vigorously opposed the Thomas-Disney bill; and although strongly recommended by various majors and independent oil men, it was defeated in the House.

The Thomas-Disney bill ruckus created enough interest in oil to cause the creation of a subcommittee of the House Interstate and Foreign Commerce Committee to investigate the industry completely.

The colonel didn't let Mr. Ickes rankle him to the extent that he lost sight of his job. His dramatic testimony and press statements against Ickes were merely a warning to any potential adversaries that he would fight back. He had made a study of the oil industry in his two years on the Commission that equipped him to cope with any petroleum economist. His faculty for finding facts was his greatest asset. He was not a man to offer an opinion or make a statement on a subject without full knowledge of all of the details and circumstances.

One reason he was so willing to accept the federal investigators in East Texas was that the Black Giant was an emergency and he needed help temporarily. The second, of course, was that his friend, Charley Francis, was to be in charge and he felt there would be no political skulduggery going on behind his back. The federal investigators also provided him with time to get some more things done.

In February of 1934 he succeeded in getting a refinery control bill through the state legislature. The bill required refineries to report the source of their crude oil. The commission had ordered such reports, but only four of sixty refineries in East Texas were complying. East Texas refineries at that time were processing 60,000 barrels of crude daily from oil wells which had aggregate allowables of 18,000 barrels. East Texas refiners marched on Austin to protest the bill and attempt to influence Governor Ferguson into a veto. She signed the bill, however, and it became the law. The refiners had claimed it would put them out of business. That was a valid claim since they could not compete without hot oil bought far below field prices. The major oil companies offered to make five percent of their own oil available to these small refiners, and that would have been ample to meet their needs, but the hot-oil refiners knew they could not compete if they had to pay posted prices for their raw product.

This refinery law was a great boon to the Commission. What the NIRA had done to reduce interstate hot oil to a bare trickle, this would do to control intrastate oil.

By mid-1934 hot oil was actually fairly well eliminated. Rumors of hot oil, however, were as strong as ever. In June Ernest Thompson was invited to attend a meeting of bankers in Dallas. Nathan Adams, president of the

First National Bank, headed a group of thirty bankers who were to meet in his bank's board room at 10 A.M. Thompson was there. For some thirty minutes Mr. Adams talked about hot oil, overproduction and what should be done in East Texas. Then he addressed his remarks directly to Thompson and asked him what was going to be done about it.

"Mr. Adams, if you will let me come up there and speak from where you just made your statements, I'll be happy to answer that and any other questions," Thompson said.

The colonel said that what Mr. Adams said was right. There was a problem in East Texas and the Commission's only interest in the problem was to see that the public was served. He pointed out that he owned no oil and no interest in oil and, therefore, had no axes to grind. Thompson told the bankers that he respected them but had no fear of them. He did say, however, that he would welcome their help.

"Gentlemen," he said, "it isn't easy to get good men, even under present conditions, for $104 a month, but you can help. If you will give me three of your bankers here in this room who will accept those jobs at that salary, I'll swear them in and they can become Commission deputies. They can act like a bank discount committee passing on loans. The other commissioners have agreed with me that these men could review each application for oil clearance before it was approved and make sure that it was pure as driven snow; as pure as a bank could make it," he added.

"We will want them to come to Kilgore every morning at 10 o'clock," he went on, "and pass on these applications so that they may issue the clearances. They can approve every application to move oil and then it will be like legal tender. Otherwise there will be no oil approved. Of course, they must approve any oil that is legally produced under the laws of Texas and the rules and regulations of the Railroad Commission."

Adams said he thought the idea was a good one and that it certainly sounded fair enough. His committee immediately prevailed upon Tucker Royall of Palestine, Walter Fair of Tyler and Walter Moore of Overton to accept the appointments to what Thompson called the "Little Commission." The men were all in banks within driving distance of Proration Hill.

Within a very few weeks they found that they were doing little or nothing. As Thompson had said, the hot oil was virtually stopped already. He was glad to get this committee because it served to stop the rumors. In their months of operation the Little Commission never found anything wrong with the operation on Proration Hill.

Later in the year Thompson reported back to the Dallas bankers with the statement that illegal oil was so hard to find in the field that the hot-oil runners had resorted to common thievery. He also said that $108 million had been added to Texas revenues by increasing allowables, and that by preventing further declines in bottom hole pressures the Commission had saved operators $9 million they were preparing to spend on standard pumping equipment.

Early in September Secretary Ickes in a public speech

blamed Texas for the ills of the oil business. He said that the state's oil wells were responsible for the nation's rapidly depleting oil reserves. Ernest Thompson could not sit by and not answer. He made a public statement in which he flayed Ickes and accused the Secretary of attempting to set himself up as an oil dictator without knowing anything about any part of the industry except its vast importance and wealth. He said the Secretary's dreams of oil dictatorship had been rudely interrupted by Texans in the state government, Texans in the national congress and Texans in the oil business. That, he said, was all Texas was to blame for and he, for his part, was proud of the accomplishment. The colonel wound up his blistering attack on the Oil Administrator by saying that, regardless of what happened in Washington, Texas would continue to take care of its own problems as long as constitutional government was recognized in this country.

In November Old Curmudgeon accepted an invitation from his good friends in the American Petroleum Institute to speak at their convention in Dallas. In the midst of a wild, arm-flinging ovation, the Oil Administrator chided the industry and its organizations while the convention delegates sat in stunned silence. Finally, he pounded on the podium and warned the industry that unless it put its house in order, and quickly, it would face either nationalization or would become classified as a public utility.

Sitting in the back of the room, Ernest Thompson nudged a friend, and made one comment.

"Well," he said with a sort of sigh of relief, "Old Ickes and federal control are both through. That speech killed them."

And it did. Within a few days most of Ickes' big-company advisors had turned against him. The oil press turned its guns on the Administrator and his Oil Code. Soon thereafter his influence began to wane. The big companies, as well as the independents, saw then and there that federal control was not all Ickes had in mind. He mentioned nationalization and a public-utility status for the entire industry. As the colonel predicted, he was through as a potential oil czar almost as of that moment.

In testifying before the Cole Committee in mid-November of 1934 Thompson listed five indications that the threat of federal control was disappearing. First, he said, major oil-company executives had admitted that the Oil Code had failed to control intrastate matters. Second, the governors-elect of Texas and Oklahoma were opposed to federal control. Allred had been made governor in Texas and Marland had won the governorship of Oklahoma. A district court in Oklahoma had held the "orderly development" section of the Oil Code invalid. That section dealt with an intrastate matter such as Ickes' attempt to direct the number of wells in Cayuga field and to stop the blowout in Conroe. He pointed out that the federal government had established a tender board which indicated an apparent inclination to adopt state enforcement methods. Thompson also said that there had been a definite change in the attitude of the Interstate Commerce Commission, once the most grasping of the federal agencies. Recently they had begun asking members of state regulatory bodies to sit in with them and take an active part in their discussions of rate cases.

The Railroad Commission's Christmas gift was a new law which gave it the power to stop the shipment of illegally produced products. It would complement the law which provided the power to prevent shipment of hot crude oil. By the end of 1934, through the combined efforts of Thompson and the federal investigators to bring about order out of chaos, the price of oil stood at a respectable ninety-five cents a barrel.

East Texas, at the end of the year, had 17,650 wells decorating its 120,000 acres. There were 700 wells within the tiny townsite of Kilgore alone, some surrounding Proration Hill. Some experts had said that $150 million had been wasted in unnecessary wells in the field.

January 7, 1935 marked the end of federal authority in East Texas. Back in May, Judge Bryant had granted the Amazon Petroleum Corporation an injunction restraining federal authorities from enforcing Section 9c of the NIRA. The circuit court had overruled the district court, but the Supreme Court had sustained Judge Bryant. In May, 1935 a small poultry dealer's case would result in the highest court declaring the entire National Recovery Administration unconstitutional four months after oil had been freed of its restrictions and protection.

On the day the Oil Code was declared unconstitutional Ernest Thompson was en route to Washington. From dozens of his friends in Texas came telegrams urging him to get off the train and return to the state as chaos would return to East Texas with the end of the federal authority. The colonel's first impulse was to return. Then he realized that his power alone was insufficient to cope with the situation so long as hot oil could move in interstate commerce. Instead, he proceeded to Washington and importuned the President to immediately submit the Connally amendment to the Oil Code as a separate law. In the meantime, he requested the attorney general of Texas to be prepared to file injunctions against any who might attempt to move untendered oil. The Texas Public Safety Department was asked to redouble its efforts to prevent hot oil from moving within the state by truck. These moves minimized the threat of chaos which might have brought about a new demand for federal control.

On February 22 the executive order that Roosevelt had issued, at Thompson's request, prior to NIRA to stop interstate shipment of hot oil, and which had later become the Connally amendment to the Oil Code, was passed as a new federal law known as the Connally Hot Oil Act.

Thompson's unswerving contention was that the government should protect states by requiring that oil entering interstate or foreign commerce be produced in accordance with state law. That, he said, was the proper province of the federal government. Any control beyond that, he added, would be an invasion of states' rights and, therefore, in violation of the constitution of the United States.

The stature of Ernest Thompson had grown considerably in the relatively short time he had been a member of the regulatory body. The new governor, James V. Allred, and the Colonel of Proration Hill were girding themselves for a more important fight. Together they had spearheaded the fight against federal control which had come from a half-dozen directions. Now they must be certain that the proposed Interstate Oil Compact Commission would not be one that would require a state to surrender some of its sovereign power.

If there were such a compact, both agreed, Texas, which was now producing as much oil as all of the other states combined, would simply be forced to remain out of it.

CHAPTER IX

Creation of the Compact

"Thompson, you're stealing my stuff."

"You're right, Mr. President, everything I have said was borrowed from one of your speeches," Ernest Thompson replied to President Roosevelt. "You see, I thought it was the best way to convey the idea about what is happening down in the oil country."

The President had greeted the colonel. The colonel had thanked Mr. Roosevelt for graciously consenting to see him. And then the colonel had, with hardly another word of explanation, launched into the speech.

For a moment Franklin Roosevelt was a bit surprised when he heard his own words coming from the Texas commissioner's mouth. They were among the most profound expressions ever made on the subject of states' rights, uttered during Roosevelt's days in Albany as Governor of New York. Then the President wanted to know what it was all about.

"Well, Mr. President, down in the Southwest we are beginning to get the idea that someone up here in Washington doesn't believe exactly as you do on this subject," Thompson said with a wisp of a smile in his fiery eyes. "At least, we know that someone up here would like to run the oil business from Washington. I know you are the captain of this ship and I thought maybe you had been led off your course a little by some one or more of your mates. I thought maybe this little refresher on the navigation would be helpful."

The President was aware of the situation. He knew that Harold Ickes was anxious to put the oil industry under control. He spent the next fifteen minutes talking with the colonel about oil. All he had heard about Thompson's vast knowledge of the industry was confirmed in that quarter of an hour. "Thompson," he finally said, "I'll tell you what you need. The oil states should have a compact. We have been in several compacts in New York and they have all benefited the industries concerned. A compact of states will work. I'll tell you what to do. You send a wire to the governors of each of the oil-producing states. Ask each of them to send two representatives to a meeting on this subject."

"I'll do that, Mr. President, but what will I do with them when they get here?" the colonel asked.

"You organize them and tell them what I have told you," Roosevelt answered, "and have them here in the cabinet room at four o'clock Monday afternoon."

"That will be about forty people, Mr. President," Ernest said, "how will I get them into the cabinet room?"

Roosevelt was amused by Thompson's typically frank inquiry. He had heard the colonel was punctilious about getting details and now here he was doing just that with the President of the United States. Roosevelt called Marvin McIntyre, his secretary, and told him of the plans and asked him to make the arrangements for the meeting.

Within an hour Thompson had sent telegrams to twenty-one governors of the states that had oil production. By early Monday there were representatives of each of the oil states registered at the Mayflower Hotel in Washington. A preliminary meeting was called by Thompson in the Chinese room and he explained what was on the President's mind. At noon the meeting was adjourned until two o'clock. The colonel took that intermission to slip over to the White House and make certain the President remembered the meeting. He told McIntyre that he had representatives of twenty-one states staked out at the Mayflower and he wanted to be certain that the cabinet room would be ready and that the President would be there. The secretary took Thompson back to see the President and Mr. Roosevelt was delighted at the complete response.

"Now, Thompson," Roosevelt explained, "I wish you would make out a card for each state delegate. At the top place the name of the state and the governor. Beneath that put the names of the two representatives. Write the names plainly. When you come into the cabinet room introduce them to me by states, and pronounce each name very clearly and correctly as you lay each card down in front of me."

Ernest Thompson got the impression from those instructions that he wasn't the only man in the country who was punctilious in planning and exacting in details. An hour or so later he brought his delegation in to meet the President and followed the instructions just as the President had given them.

At the meeting Mr. Roosevelt spoke at some length

about the need for waste prevention. Occasionally he
glanced over to Thompson who, he knew, was thinking
without saying it how Mr. Roosevelt was using Mr.
Thompson's stuff this time.

"What you gentlemen need is an oil-states compact in
order to eliminate the complaint I hear so often of inconsistent and even contradictory regulations," Roosevelt told the assemblage. "Thompson here tells me that
you want to avoid any form of federal control. You
work out a compact and that may do the trick. I'll help
you do it."

Ernest Thompson and the other men left the President's cabinet room with the feeling that Roosevelt was
a strong advocate of the sovereignty of states.

That meeting followed the Governors Oil Conference
by several weeks and preceded a second conference that
followed in Washington for the next several days. It
happened, too, several weeks before Congress passed the
NIRA and the famous Oil Code went into effect. The
NIRA put a sudden halt to all discussions about an oil
compact.

The idea of an oil-states compact was not new. In
fact, another famous New Yorker, Elihu Root, had suggested it as early as 1910 during his term as a United
States senator. In 1931, with East Texas menacing the
industry, the governors of Texas, Kansas, Oklahoma
and New Mexico met in Fort Worth to name an Oil
States Advisory Committee. Early in 1932 their representatives met in Austin and a preliminary draft of a
Uniform Legislative Act for Conservation and Interstate
Compact was drawn up. The idea was not original with

the colonel but none had previously seen it with the same clear vision as he.

On December 3, 1934, the governors of the oil-producing states met with Governor-elect Marland of Oklahoma in his vast mansion just outside of Ponca City to discuss an interstate oil compact. Marland had long sought legislation to permit such a law. He had fought for it in congress and now, with the end of the NIRA in sight, he was taking up the fight again. But Marland's idea was in conflict with that of Texans. Marland's plan would give the signatories to the compact the authority to fix prices and set production quotas by states, fields and even wells. It would have had the effect of eliminating much of the authority of the various state regulatory bodies. To many in the oil industry, Marland seemed inconsistent. He fought the NIRA because it provided an opening wedge for permanent federal control. He fought the big companies and what he termed "the money trust" because it would dictate to and squeeze out, as he put it, every little man in the business. Now he wanted a form of state compact that Ernest Thompson was certain would lead to both federal control and monopoly. In fact, Marland's proposal actually would give the federal government equal representation with the states. It would allocate domestic production to each state. The proposal went so far as to determine the amount of oil and products that could be produced and shipped from any state in interstate commerce.

When Governor-elect Allred returned from the Marland meeting he called Colonel Thompson to his office and explained the Marland compact plan. He said he would have none of it, and Thompson readily agreed. On January 3, just three days before the Supreme Court ended the NRA, there was another meeting of the oil governors in Ponca City. At this meeting Allred informed the assembled governors and state regulatory members that Texas would not go along with the Marland plan. Texas was willing, however, to enter a compact which would leave the states free to meet and discuss their common problems and to arrive at intelligent solutions. But Texas would never enter a compact which would mean the surrender of a single power of any sovereign state. That was the way they left it with Marland. A meeting was called for February 16 in Dallas at which the matter would be finally discussed.

In the meantime Ernest Thompson's remarkable contribution to his state in controlling the great East Texas field and stabilizing the industry was the occasion for a testimonial dinner at the Baker Hotel in Dallas. It also celebrated his recent election to the Commission chairmanship.

There some of the industry's stalwarts and hundreds of Thompson's friends met to honor the colonel. He was praised for his effective fight against federal control and particularly against the Thomas-Disney bill. Carl Calloway, Thompson's old campaign manager, recalled an incident of a few months back when Thompson called on a committee clerk to get a copy of the Thomas-Disney bill which was coming off the duplicating machine. The clerk had been instructed not to give the colonel a copy because he would raise too much hell.

"They are right, young man," Thompson had told the

clerk, "I'll raise hell if you give it to me, but you go back to your committee chairman and tell him I intend to raise a damn sight more hell if they don't."

"The clerk came back with a copy," Calloway said. "This man Thompson risked, even invited, political suicide opposing an administration bill at the time President Roosevelt was riding the highest crest of popularity any President in this country has ever known."

Elwood Fouts, outstanding Houston oil attorney and advisor to Governor Allred, told of his early misgivings about Thompson. "He had to prove himself to me," said Fouts, "because I had been told he was the biggest crook ever to hold office in Texas. I was completely prejudiced against him when I first met him. But I was happy to find that he was a redhead because I believed he would fight. But then I saw him back off a fight with a disarming smile and some witticism and I figured I had misjudged my man. Frankly, I believed he was yellow. What I had to learn was that he had control of temper rather than lack of it."

Fouts then told of the trips to Washington he had made with Thompson and how quixotic the cause they were defending seemed to him.

"But the success which came in the end again proved how wrong I was about this man," Fouts said, turning to smile at the colonel. Then he said that he believed Thompson had rendered greater service to Texas than any man in the generation.

John Boyles, San Antonio attorney who had once been in favor of some kind of federal control and completely opposed to Thompson, told of the great debt the state owed the new chairman. He also told of the high regard the members of the congressional committees had for Thompson.

But the testimonial that touched the colonel more than any other came from his colleague, Judge C. V. Terrell, who said:

"He has been on the Commission with me for three years, and he has done my work, lifted my burden, helped me, and helped the people of Texas. I know of no man in Texas to whom the people of this State, in fact this nation, owe more than they owe to Colonel Ernest O. Thompson. I am going to say this. In all of my varied experience with men, I know of no man I hold higher than Colonel Thompson. I know of no man who is as keen, as bright, or has a mind as alert as that of Colonel Thompson. Every citizen of Texas should be proud of him."

It was only a few days after this meeting that Governor Allred asked Fouts to talk with Thompson about the proposed Interstate Oil Compact. Allred told both men that he had no intention of following the ideas of Governor Marland because he considered the prime purpose of the Oklahoma plan to be one of price-fixing. Marland's price-fixing was probably based on his sympathy for the stripper well operators who were numerous in his state as well as in Kansas, Pennsylvania, Indiana, West Virginia and New York. But the Texans were of the opinion that there was no such thing as a little price-fixing and that before long, if such a policy were pursued, federal control and monopoly would completely envelop the industry.

Elwood Fouts was a remarkable man and an uncompromising champion of states' rights. Even when Thompson himself veered slightly off the course and into the edge of the shadow of price-fixing for marginal wells, Fouts steered him straight. Between the two men the logic of their approach was one of magnificent simplicity.

As finally drafted for the approval of Governor Allred, the compact provided merely for a treaty between oil-producing states to prevent waste. It provided for the prevention of physical waste and a definition of the major causes of such waste. It provided for the voluntary co-operation of the oil-producing states in promoting good conservation practices. It specified that, of course, those objectives were minimums and were not intended in any way to limit the scope of any member-state's authority.

It provided that those minimums be enacted by the various state legislatures within a reasonable time. It specifically pointed out that the limits put on production of oil and gas by the joining states would not be imposed for the purpose of price-fixing, the creation or perpetuation of monopoly, or to promote regimentation. It further provided that the compact should expire at the end of two years, but that any state could withdraw from the compact within sixty days.

The four states that had long sought such a compact, Texas, Oklahoma, Kansas and New Mexico, plus California, were included in the Thompson-Fouts proposal. Provision was made, however, that when the legislatures of any three states ratified the measure, the compact would become effective.

When the meeting was held in Dallas on February 16, Oklahoma came prepared to push the Marland plan. There were numerous attempts to sell the Oklahoma idea to the other states in meetings. A strong plea was made by Marland and others, and much pressure was put on Allred to change his stand. All were to no avail. When Allred got up to offer the Texas plan he said that his state would, under no circumstances, enter into any compact that abrogated the rights of or invaded, even in the slightest degree, the sovereignty of any other state. Marland decided to take Pat Hurley's advice and first get a compact and then work on the details. Thompson suggested that Marland be made the first chairman of the Interstate Oil Compact. That was a master stroke since it took most of the opposition out of the Oklahoman. He was, by virtue of his long devotion to the cause, in personal time and expense, probably the true pioneer of an oil-states compact. Many times in the future Thompson would refer to him as the father of the compact. But the details Hurley said he could add later were never added. Years later the compact, authored by Thompson and Fouts, and pushed with unrelenting determination by Allred, remained in its original form.

The immediate reaction within the industry was that the compact, as it was presented by the Texans and as passed by Congress six months later, was an ineffective scrap of paper without power and almost without purpose. All it provided was that representatives of oil-producing states would meet and discuss their common problems and attempt to arrive at some uniform solution. The compact would, of course, provide a medium for the exchange of ideas and the advancement of technological, scientific, governmental and other progress.

Congressman William Cole of Maryland, who was seriously concerned with the ills of the oil industry, headed a subcommittee of the House Interstate and Foreign Commerce Committee. The initial purpose of his subcommittee seemed to be to support the claims for the need of federal controls, since he had once sponsored a federal control bill himself. The committee traveled to almost every oil-producing state in the nation. In fact, it was present in Ponca City for the birth of the modern oil compact.

When the committee made its report back to Congress, it recommended that federal control was not indicated by its findings but that a law to authorize the creation of an interstate oil compact was needed immediately. Marland, Thompson, Allred and others were witnesses for the bill. Wirt Franklin, the IPAA man, favored "stronger controls," and A. A. Seeligson of San Antonio testified that ninety percent of the oil men wanted federal control. The congress passed the Interstate Oil Compact Law in August of 1935.

Governor Allred appointed the colonel as his representative on the compact. In spite of its lack of power, except, as Thompson described it, "the power of public opinion," he was able to report in 1936 that the compact had helped defeat federal control, won the support of both the independents and the majors, was prepared to submit uniform conservation laws, had been instrumental in aiding the Bureau of Mines with counsel and assistance in getting adequate appropriations, and had brought about a climate of mutual trust within the oil-producing states.

What he did not report was that the knowledge, statesmanship, leadership and influence of Ernest O. Thompson had, far more than the petulant Marland or any others, provided the oil that had quieted the troubled waters of the petroleum industry, largely through the medium of the Interstate Oil Compact.

CHAPTER X

The People Approve

On the afternoon of October 10, 1935, Colonel Thompson delivered an address at the annual meeting of the American Petroleum Institute at Los Angeles. Most of its members were representatives of the major oil companies. The relations between some of these companies and the Texas Railroad Commission had not been cordial since the discovery of the East Texas oil field and the occasion had a little of the flavor of Daniel walking into the lion's den. At least that is how the colonel felt about it.

He heard the usual laudatory introduction and he wished it were possible for him to believe the API men believed the nice things the master of ceremonies had said. He felt that he had been invited here because he was now chairman of the Texas Railroad Commission and that his position called for reluctant respect from the oil companies. Ernest Thompson had his speech in mind. He wondered if it would do what he wanted it to do. He wanted it to remove doubt and suspicion from this important segment of the industry. He wanted these men to know exactly where they stood.

The colonel had stood between the same companies

and East Texas. They had hoped to be able to dictate the policies in the field which had been found and largely developed by independents before all of the integrated companies awoke to what was happening. He had blocked their plan for an appointive State Conservation Commission that could be easily dominated. The colonel had also thwarted the small band of big-company men who had tried to bring about federal control. Before the voters of Texas and before the congressional committees in Washington and in public statements to the press he had expressed himself openly about the sin of monopoly and the fact that he believed certain big oil-company leaders were anxious to control the industry.

He opened his talk with an appeal to API members to refrain from selling oil to Japan or any other country for war purposes. That opening was probably designed to put some of his bitter critics at ease for a moment. Then he slid into second gear by touching lightly on his assigned subject, "Proration Laws and Their Application in Texas."

The colonel is a patient man and courtesy is almost a fetish with him. But above both of those traits is his quality of forthrightness. He had no desire to offend anyone, but he did want these men to understand him. For a few minutes he discussed the problems of the Commission. He told of the oil situation in Texas. And he described the newest techniques of drilling and exploration in the state. Soon he had the audience, many of its members oil men who had never seen an oil well, hypnotized with his discussion of field geology and engineering. As he spoke the audience's respect for his intelligence and integrity grew. Now, he sensed, was the time to get in the first important point.

"Because Texas is the greatest oil-producing state, her public policy is of great importance to the oil industry, and that policy should be understood with all possible sympathy by each of you," he said.

"In the bill of rights of our state constitution monopolies are prohibited in the following language: 'Perpetuities and monopolies are contrary to the genius of a free government, and shall never be allowed.'

"Our statute books are full of laws designed and intended to make this fundamental policy effective. It was never intended by the people of Texas that giant corporations should grow up in the oil industry or any other industry and be permitted to exercise a destroying hand or exert harmful influence over the economic life of our people."

The audience stirred slightly. Many felt they were now in for a frontal attack that would teach the board of directors to be more careful in the selection of speakers. The colonel looked at the audience, many of whom had worked against his efforts.

"Our hope and our purpose is always to preserve opportunities in the economic life of our state for our children. We want them to have the privilege of doing the same things that many of you have done—start from scratch and rise to a place of power and wealth in the industry. Sometimes you may forget, the richest and most powerful of you, that you had a small beginning. You could never have accomplished what you have if it had not been for the shelter and protection you received from our government against the selfishness and greed of others more powerful."

That was the keynote to his real subject. If it had its effect, Texas policy was made plain and all could be guided by it. If there were any present who felt the remarks hit close to home, those were the men the colonel had hoped would hear them.

He went on to say that the Commission's rules were fair, though imperfect, and that good results had been obtained.

"They are usually viewed in the light of one's own particular interest and the viewpoint depends on whose ox is being gored," he said.

He told them that industry and science were making great strides in understanding "this valuable but fugacious product placed underground by nature." Then he said the Commission was willing and ready to adjust to meet advances as facts and information become available.

"But we intend for all to play the game according to the rules. There are enough opportunities and ample resources for all in this great nation. If you, the greatest, will understand that there are others as deserving coming along to take your places, and if you will not begrudge them the same rare privilege you have enjoyed, we will all be happier. Our burden on the Commission will be lighter and you will help simplify our task of dealing fairly, intelligently and honestly with all concerned."

He reminded his listeners that the stricter the Commission prorated, the lower the allowables became and the more wells were drilled and, consequently, the further it was necessary to again reduce allowables. He said it was a vicious merry-go-round with him and his colleagues in the middle trying to keep the organ in tune.

He said federal control was a dead issue because the general public was not interested. Gasoline prices had not increased in fifteen years and oil reserves were ample. If prices were exorbitant or if oil reserves were short the public might have been on the Ickes-oil-company band wagon of federal control, he said.

"The desire for federal control came from within the industry," he said, looking about the room. Almost every man in the industry who had sought federal control was within earshot of his voice. "Then the industry made a rapid reversal. It found the price it was asked to pay for controls was too high. That price was bureaucrats interfering in matters of marketing, labor relations, refinery, pipeline and production operations. And there was the promise of a public-utility status for you. That was the price. Had it not been for a few Texans who were more interested in the right of our state to run its own business, that price would have been paid by now, too. You woke up just in time in Dallas."

He reminded his audience that people experiment with radical social legislation only in times of emergency, and that at present times were getting better. Therefore, there would be no federal control. He didn't mention Ickes or the industry leaders who had worked hand in hand with him.

The colonel, without glancing at a note, recited a half-dozen court opinions almost verbatim. His vast knowledge of the law and the constitution was amazing. He then told what Texas expected of the industry.

"Texas wants a good price for crude oil. Oil is our leading industry. Our commercial life is stimulated by its prosperity. Our schools, the income of our people, and the revenues with which to operate our State depend on it. Texas wants oil and other industries for our people to engage in. Our people also want us to see that independent oil men are not eliminated."

When the colonel ended his speech with an appeal for understanding and co-operation in a job that would benefit the industry as well as the people of the entire nation, the audience broke into a deafening ovation. Like a wave moving toward the back of the room the oil men stood and cheered the man who had been so frank and honest and intelligent in his discussion with them. Ernest Thompson was surprised by the unexpected reaction. He knew now that he had won the fight he had been waging. For if the majors understood his philosophy and his state's policy, most of his troubles would be over. These men realized that Thompson was no political hack trying to make a hit with the folks back home, but a man who could pull America's only native and most typical industry out of its fog of mistrust and misunderstanding.

Ernest Thompson's leadership in the oil industry began the day Ross Sterling appointed him to the Railroad Commission. It was recognized early by the honest independents in the East Texas field when he became their champion. The colonel believed that as a public official it was his duty to protect the little men in the industry, those who were attempting to live within the law. Congressional committees recognized him as an impartial spokesman who had a vast knowledge of the industry, its economics, politics and techniques. At the organization meeting of the Interstate Oil Compact his devotion to states' rights was recognized; in fact this had already been expressed before Congress in his fight on federal controls. His consistency was amazing. Now the last obstacle had been hurdled. The majors saw in Thompson the kind of leadership the industry had long needed. Their opposition to state control had not necessarily been born of a desire to create monopoly. It had been based on the fact that up until this moment they had not found a political leader in the states with the many qualifications necessary to the job. But here, in Thompson, was the man. They knew that he would influence the Texas Railroad Commission as long as he was a part of it and they knew that Texas, as long as it dominated the oil producing industry, would vastly influence the national petroleum scene.

Thompson's patience had outlasted the loudest and the angriest men in the industry. He was the first man who had approached his problem from the standpoint of the interest of the general public knowing that its first need was for a constant supply of oil and gas; its second, for a fair price of the product; and its third, the health of an industry which had become essential to American economy. All of these interests called for a balanced industry. Now for the first time in its history, it seemed that the boom-and-bust days, the days of feast and famine in the oil industry were over. Gone were the production orgies of Ranger, Burkburnett, El Dorado and Seminole; the ghost towns that succeeded boom towns. East Texas was the turning point, and Ernest Thompson was its guiding star. Hereafter oil fields would become permanent towns, clean and prosperous, where people could live in peace and security. Where there were no towns, field camps would grow up with the emphasis on schools, churches, recreation halls and parks instead of gambling dens, bawdyhouses, saloons and street-fighting. These were the outward signs of change. But the difference went deeper. The turbulence of the old days that meant demoralizing and wanton loss of reservoirs resulting from the ruthless and rapid withdrawals by men bent on sudden fortunes would be supplanted by slow and sensible drainage that would give the oil sands the full measure of their lives in which to give up the full measure of their bounty.

The trouble was not all over, but the enlightenment that came with the influence of Ernest Thompson would continue to spread. Thompson was not the first man who had wanted this new order. He was simply the first man who had the intelligence, patience, perserverance and fearless determination to bring it about.

In 1935 the end of the troublemakers was in sight. The die-hard executives of the few big companies who felt that their only defense against cutthroat competition was the freeze-out, and the unscrupulous independents who sought wealth at any price were on the way out. A new type of competition was born. It was about that time that men in the oil industry started calling their business "the oil fraternity." The problems of each segment became the problems of the other segments. A sense of moral and public responsibility began to permeate the industry.

There would still be men in the industry who would damn and villify Ernest Thompson and the other leaders who believed as he did, but with each passing day more and more men in and out of the industry would recognize the voice of Ernest Thompson as that of the true spokesman for the industry whether it was in the halls of Congress, at the oil compact meetings, before civic organizations, political gatherings, or the hundreds of industry organizations. It was a firm voice, plain, simple and effective, with no undertone of selfish motive or personal interest.

By the end of 1935 Texas was not only the greatest oil-producing state in the nation, but the colonel's home country in the Panhandle had developed into the most prolific natural-gas country in the world. Therein rested another problem. The vast Panhandle gas field had become the center of another battle between the big operators and the little independents. Again the colonel was found on the side of the little men.

In his four years on the Railroad Commission Thompson had been confronted with innumerable gas-utility decisions and he had instituted changes resulting in savings of almost two million dollars a year for the consumers. For the first time the state had engaged expert evaluation men to match those of the utility companies, just as Thompson had done in Amarillo. He had killed off the management fees utility companies paid to

Eastern holding companies as a rate consideration. He stopped gas-utility companies from charging the operation of their appliance business as an expense to be considered in rate matters. Thompson did not believe that the public, including other appliance dealers, should be penalized by higher gas rates resulting from the operating expenses for the utilities companies' appliance business. And, finally, he had said that service-club participation and other civic activity did not constitute legitimate expenses for rate making. He agreed that the utility men should participate most actively in civic affairs but he did not agree that their customers should pay for that participation. In his quiet approach, most of these things were actually overlooked by the public. They all came from his experiences in Amarillo. Once, however, in Santa Anna, he had been instrumental in raising rates for a utility company that was losing money and that action was heralded around the State by his critics, who were legion.

As 1936 rolled around the colonel was confronted with the problem of running for office again. He had already served on the Commission longer than he had expected to, but his job was far from complete. The challenge was still there and many in the oil industry were visibly perturbed over the slight possibility that he might not choose to run again. He talked the matter over with May, who would have chosen to return to Amarillo where the colonel could give more attention to his own properties, none of which were oil, if she had her way. Both, however, agreed that he should stay with the Commission at least another two or three years.

Ernest Thompson was by far the most controversial figure who had ever served on the Texas Railroad Commission. He was his own master in all situations. He had no political boss and no faction that could or would attempt to steer him. In almost every important move the Commission had taken since 1933 he had been the spearhead. He had assumed leadership, spoken freely on all issues when questioned, taken a firm stand on anything he believed to be in the public interest. He had made thousands of important decisions based on his own complete fact-finding. Almost always Judge Terrell had gone along with him. Frequently the decisions had been unanimous. The citizens of Texas had never had an opportunity to express themselves on his policies. He believed they were entitled to a chance to do so and that belief had a great bearing on his decision to run for re-election.

There was one major discordant note in his decision. He knew that Lon A. Smith, his colleague, would doubtlessly oppose him. Thompson and Terrell had ruled against clients of Smith's son in order to protect the Commission's reputation for integrity. Smith had resented the action of his colleagues and Thompson knew that reprisals would result. He was more concerned with the effect on the Commission and on Judge Terrell than he was with his own welfare but he hoped that the 1936 race could be decisive since it was a policy rather than a man that was on trial.

In this political battle he would face three types of opposition. First, he would be opposed by several important utilities who had cases brought by the Commission in court. These cases had been brought largely by Thompson and his vigor would carry them through to a conclusion. With him out of the picture, they might hope for relief. Many such cases were tied up in court by dilatory tactics of utility lawyers who hoped for a Thompson defeat. Then, a very few major company executives who had been whipped down by Thompson on federal control, acreage proration, and lesser individual battles, were anxious to see him defeated. The third set of opponents were the powerful hot oil runners, many of whom had built up tremendous wealth before the advent of Thompson and whose fortunes were suffering from his rigorous enforcement.

The other candidates in the race seemed to be no great threat. One was a perennial candidate for state office who seemed to run for the sake of running. A second, Thompson described as a disgruntled state employee who advocated "fair recognition of women in the conduct of the state's affairs." Another was a former state senator who had been friendly with the utility companies opposed to Thompson. The fourth candidate was Frank Morris, a lawyer and wartime district attorney.

The colonel opened his race at Alvord, in Wise County, the town of his birth. Thousands gathered from all over the state. People came from the colonel's home country of the Panhandle, from East Texas, the Gulf Coast, the Rio Grande Valley and far West Texas. His speech was the culmination of a full day of activity including a parade, a band concert and a typical Texas barbecue.

The barbecue was managed by John Snyder of Amarillo, the rotund "Barbecue King of the Panhandle" and a man who had worked for the colonel years before in his hotels. One of John's pre-speech quotes that day made its way around the state.

"He pays good wages and he feeds well. There ain't nobody ever made no mistake no time voting for Ernest Thompson."

The crowd was full of grateful independents, a good scattering of friendly major company men, some of the utility executives who had co-operated with the Commission's rate reductions, railroad leaders from both management and labor, and thousands of old friends from everywhere. The boys from the 90th Division seemed to have come in from every nook and cranny of the state. Alvord was never more proud of a citizen than it was of its native son, the fighting colonel of the Meuse-Argonne, the battling mayor of Amarillo and the colorful captain of Proration Hill. Wherever he went he was cheered, slapped on the back, and urged to "give 'em hell," an old Texas campaign war cry.

Judge Terrell, himself a native of Wise County, introduced the colonel and told the home folks that he was the greatest Texan in public office since Jim Hogg. The judge spoke of Ernest's integrity, his intelligence and energy.

The colonel's speech was a remarkable treatise on the accomplishments of the Commission. Never did he refer to his own personal leadership. He spoke of the three-man body as if it were an individual.

"This Commission has fought for the right of the

people of Texas to control our own internal affairs in oil and gas productions," he said by way of explaining the fight against federal control. "My race," he continued in the only personal reference of the day, "should decide whether we have truly represented the people's views in this matter."

He attacked the evils of the past fifty years as practised by a few of the large companies and bore down on imports at a time of overproduction of domestic oil, and the old practice of making heavy withdrawals from storage while purchasing oil from independents at depressed prices.

The reckless independents who flaunted the Commission's production orders were called the greatest menace to the public interest.

Anticipating, as he did, the Smith attack and those by some of the victims of his energetic enforcement policy, both majors and independents, he said "If you hear the tongues of slander, go behind the slanderous words to their motive. You will find men who asked special favors and were denied; men who opposed, ineffectually, the actions we determined were for the best interests of the most people."

He told of the Commission's fight for lower gas rates, drought freight rates for cotton farmers and ranchers, and he explained why there had to be proration.

"Without proration the price of crude oil and gasoline would drop and the people would enjoy cheap fuel like a spendthrift running through an inheritance. But when the oil was gone in a few months or years, gasoline prices would soar beyond the reach of the average man."

Through more than an hour of scholarly discussion mingled with a touch of political dramatics here and there, Ernest Thompson held his listeners spellbound. When he came to the end his audience rewarded him with a tremendous ovation.

That was his big speech of the first Democratic primary. It was reprinted over the state in newspapers and pamphlets. The colonel devoted most of the remainder of the campaign to visiting around the state and repeating parts of his Alvord speech when he had time away from his duties.

When the votes were counted Thompson had carried 243 of the state's 254 counties and he had 278,000 votes more than Morris, his nearest opponent. But he lacked 9839 votes, a scant two percent of the total, of having a clear majority over the field. Morris could withdraw, which he was inclined to do in view of the overwhelming Thompson lead, or he could enter the second primary run-off. Thompson's enemies, fully aware that they could not defeat him, nevertheless, talked Morris into making the run-off race so they could continue to heap abuse on the man who had made their lives miserable. It was actually a spite campaign.

The colonel and his friends saw it for what it was. They planned a campaign, but intended to call on Thompson for only one major speech.

Early in the campaign Lon Smith had issued a damning pamphlet in which he accused the colonel of being determined to rule or ruin the Commission. He said Thompson was aligned with the monopolists and the utilities. Smith claimed that the proration orders in East

Texas were ruining the industry and especially many of the small independents. He even charged that some of the colonel's appointees were guilty of malfeasance in office. And he had urged voters to cast their votes for anyone except Thompson.

This attack, coming from a colleague, was most serious. It went even further than the colonel ever expected his fellow commissioner to go. It implicated Terrell and was a threat to the conservation program that was beginning to pay off for the industry and the state. Smith did not mention a single good thing the colonel had accomplished.

Four days before the election Ernest yielded to the pleas of his friends and went on the air to answer the charges on a state-wide radio network.

"One cannot meet the cold steel of character assassination with kid gloves," he shouted into the microphone. From that point on he pulled out all of the stops in a rebuttal to the Smith pamphlet. He told in exact detail the story of Smith's son and how he and Terrell had importuned their colleague to dissuade the young man from practicing before the Commission, how Smith had refused, and the steps they had been required to take. He called the pro-monopolist charge ridiculous and recalled his fights against monopoly. He produced a letter, signed by Smith, urging the utility companies to aid in the fight against Thompson. Then he revealed how Freeman Burford, an independent who had been a Thompson supporter in 1932, had turned against him because he would not clear large quantities of Burford's oil produced without Commission authority. Burford, he said, had threatened to beat Thompson in 1936 and he suggested that this man, who had only recently become one of the largest stockholders in a major oil company, was Smith's chief financial backer.

Thompson went on to charge that his opponent was backed by producers of unlawful oil, illegal truckers, and the utilities who had been and were opposing the Commission's orders. He pointed out that in the first primary he had beaten Morris two-to-one in Morris' own 29th Judicial District where he had once been a district attorney, and had beaten him nine-to-one in Thompson's home stable in the Panhandle.

The speech was forceful but not venomous. At the beginning and at the end of the talk he expressed his reluctance to answer the Smith charges. He also said he felt sorry for Smith who had erred. For the first time in his life he had publicly recognized and taken the defensive against political mudslinging. His friends had believed it necessary for him to answer the damaging charges.

When the votes were counted it was a three-to-one victory for Thompson. The people had vindicated the man and the policies of the Commission. It was the first test of the issue of proration and other conservation matters ever put to the voters. The results strengthened not only Thompson the commissioner and his policies, but the entire philosophy of the conservation of natural resources.

CHAPTER XI

The Biscuit Avalanche

Ernest Thompson was proud of his victory in the second Democratic primary which was, of course, confirmed with the usual party landslide in the general election in November. In spite of Lon Smith's unique opposition from within the Commission itself, the victory at the polls had been resounding.

During late 1936 and early 1937 there was a slight recession from the normal upswing of the Roosevelt recovery program. The President's election to a second term over the Kansas oilman and ex-governor, Alf Landon, had been about as one-sided as Thompson's general election margin. The colonel saw a new demand for oil coming about and spent much of his time attempting to quiet the fears of men in the industry.

One day in a state-wide proration hearing in Austin he listened to as much pessimism as he could stand and then took the oilmen to task. He reminded them that their situation in relation to other businesses had steadily improved for the past five years, that demand for oil was going up, and that prices were firm. A master of statistics and one of the few men in the world who can make cold figures sound as fascinating as a detective story, he brought his audience to its senses. He said they should be thankful that they were in the one business that had suffered no decline since the depression but had steadily advanced, especially in Texas, and had an even brighter future.

In the spring, President Roosevelt called Ernest from Washington to ask whether or not he would accept an appointment as his personal representative to the second World Petroleum Congress to be held in Paris in mid-June of 1937. Ernest was delighted. Roosevelt said he believed Thompson was the logical man to represent the President of the United States.

"After all, Thompson," the President said, "I hear from everyone in the industry and in government that you are the most effective oil regulator in the country. And not too long ago, the people in Texas said the same thing even more forcefully than I can say it."

The next few weeks were spent on routine matters. The colonel was now the chairman of the Interstate Oil Compact, having succeeded Governor Marland. He attended a meeting shortly before leaving for Europe, and it seemed that all of the states were satisfied with the way things were going.

Ernest's staff for the Paris meeting consisted solely of his technical adviser, R. W. Byram, a wiry man with a small moustache and a steel-trap mind. Byram was an engineer and conducted an oil statistical bureau in Austin. He filled two trunks full of charts, graphs, maps and statistics. Most of them were his own, but the colonel provided many official documents from Commission and Compact files. May went along to be with Ernest and to renew her old friendships on the Continent where she had scored many operatic hits in the years gone by.

In Paris the Thompson party established its headquarters at the Hotel Georges V where he had first stayed with Judge Gaines in 1914. As the representative of the President of the United States he was naturally sought out by the leaders of other governments. His reputation as soldier as well as an oil administrator had preceded him, and military leaders also flocked to his suite. He found that Europeans considered war inevitable and that plans were already under way to stock-pile petroleum. He conferred with western European leaders on the types of petroleum necessary for various defense operations, and the strategic disposition of oil stocks to serve most effectively in the event of war.

The colonel found the petroleum situation in Europe one that offered great opportunity to his state's market. There was only one well in England and it had produced less than 100,000 barrels in 1936. In France members of the Schlumberger family showed him wells that were dug like water wells on Texas farms and produced about as efficiently. That was the extent of France's oil. Germany had a fair amount of production and was progressing seriously in the field of petroleum synthetics. Rumania was the leading oil nation in Europe but the entire country yielded less oil than the Conroe field on the Texas Gulf Coast. Russia actually had by far the greatest oil potential and production on the continent. But all of the thirty-two nations represented by 1600 scientists were anxious to start oil developments. Their trouble was that they lacked the climate necessary to such a program. Minerals in every other nation in the world were nationalized. Individuals had little incentive to risk the capital necessary for oil. Governments themselves lacked the imagination or even a willingness to co-operate. Foreign markets were throttled by such restrictions as a tax of thirty-nine cents a gallon on gasoline in France with a fixed price of forty-three cents for the wholesaler and fifty-four cents for the retailer.

Several of the colonel's friends at the Congress utilized their time stirring up foreign markets for Texas crude oil. The colonel watched a French ship unload Texas Oil from Corpus Christi. He toured the refinery where the oil was sent and was permitted to study their plant-recovery records, costs, distribution and other details. He offered many valuable suggestions for improvement and received the grateful thanks of the refinery manager.

The Congress was a meeting of scientists and government leaders. Ernest addressed one of the meetings and spoke in French. His own knowledge of the language had been supplemented on the ship and in Paris by May, who spoke French fluently. His speech was a masterpiece of statistical information. The Europeans were amazed at the number of American independent operators. The information about the vast reserve, the strict regulations, and the individual ownership struck most of the delegates as incredible. While he spoke, Byram was distributing copies of the colonel's speech to the audience. It was printed in English, French, Spanish, Italian and German.

The colonel learned at the meeting that Europe could easily use a minimum 100,000 barrels of Texas oil a day.

When he returned home he advocated that operators who developed their own foreign markets should be permitted extra allowables as an incentive for salesmanship so long as the allowables did not interfere with good conservation practices. His colleagues agreed with the plan. He warned, however, that military leaders were expecting a war within two years and that he hoped oil from this country could prove an economic aid that might avert war. Under no conditions would oil allowables be given for purposes of war stock-piling for aggressor nations.

If Ernest Thompson harbored any resentment against Lon Smith for his participation in the 1936 campaign, he failed to make any outward indication of the fact. Smith remained a bit surly and cool toward Thompson, but the colonel was as cordial and typically polite to Smith as he had been the first day he went on the Commission. That, incidentally, was one of the colonel's traits that usually worried his opponents and critics. Whatever his feelings might be, he was able to maintain the external appearance of courteous, even warm, relations. But in spite of this Smith continued to resent his one to two minority position on the Commission. He rarely missed an opportunity to criticize orders signed by Thompson and Terrell. He seemed to entertain the hope that Terrell might be eliminated from the Commission in 1938, and that his successor might see things as Smith saw them.

In 1937 Smith objected to an order shutting down the East Texas field on Sundays. Thompson said the weekly shutdown was for the purpose of checking pressures, and the engineers actually did that; but Smith said it was for the purpose of holding prices in line at the expense of East Texas operators. Tom Foster, publisher of the *Kilgore News*, agreed with Smith and contended that the shutdowns would result in Terrell's defeat in 1938. Foster called the shutdowns a subterfuge and said his interest was in the loss of $427,000 in royalties to land-owners and of 2,300,000 barrels of oil on the four Sundays covered by the order.

Tom Foster's hint was not taken seriously by anyone, especially the colonel who could not conceive of anyone voting against the grand old man of the Commission. Probably if Thompson had considered the Foster proph-ecy more seriously he would have come closer to sub-duing a burning ambition that he himself had.

The colonel felt that he had rendered good service to his state, and that the people had shown their attitude toward him in the 1936 election. It might have been the day he decided to run for mayor of Amarillo, or the day he accepted the appointment to the Railroad Commis-sion, or some time right after his overwhelming 1936 victory, but somewhere in the past he had decided he wanted to be the governor of Texas. He considered it the highest political gift in the hands of the people and a reward the electorate held out for a job well done. He wanted the honor, and he felt that he could render great service to his state. He probably believed that such service could ultimately result in even higher political achievements, and by late 1936 it seems that the political bug had taken a pretty good bite out of him.

The one obstacle on the horizon in late 1937 was the

attorney general of Texas, another redhead, William C. McCraw of Dallas. To many Texans, McCraw was the natural candidate. The attorney general's office was the most common stepping stone to the big white colonial governor's mansion across the street from the massive, native granite replica of the national capitol that served as the capitol of the Lone Star State. McCraw was a brilliant lawyer who had been criminal prosecuting attorney in Dallas with a remarkable record of achievement. Like Thompson, he was a World-War-I officer. His law partner was Tom Clark, a man who was destined to become attorney general of the United States and associate justice of the Supreme Court.

The only other block in his path was Governor James V. Allred who had developed a bitter, but unexplained distaste for McCraw. Allred had actually encouraged Thompson to seek the governorship but had then become concerned over the fact that Thompson might not be able to handle the rough and tumble McCraw whose almost professional wit was capable of swinging audiences. When Allred, from an interview in Mexico late in 1937, started a boom by saying he thought Roosevelt should be a candidate in 1940 for a third term, Thompson took this as an indication that possibly Allred had decided to ignore the two-term tradition in Texas himself and run against McCraw. There was much talk of Allred's determination to stop McCraw even if he had to buck tradition and ride in on his own tremendous popularity.

The colonel heard much of this talk. He called Allred immediately upon his return from Mexico to check on whether or not the governor had serious third-term aspirations. Allred denied the rumor and Ernest then informed him that he himself would announce at a minute after midnight on January 1, 1938. The colonel's flair for the dramatic was as sharp as ever. Actually, many think this action by Thompson had a great deal to do with Allred's staying out of the race. It might have also had something to do with the governor's growing coolness toward the Thompson campaign, although he continued to back Thompson.

Besides McCraw, who had been running for governor unofficially for years, there were other contestants. Tom Hunter, who ran just behind Ma Ferguson and Governor Sterling in 1932 and had been runner-up to Allred in both of his races, was considered a formidable candidate. There were nine other assorted and relatively insignificant entries in the race.

On May 1, actually very late for an announcement, Wilbert Lee O'Daniel, native of Ohio, flour salesman extraordinary and star of the famous Lightcrust Doughboys hillbilly musical organization, and radio idol of the rural folk in Texas, announced that he had succumbed to a great popular demand and had decided to make the sacrifice and offer for governor. He said his decision was based on the response to his Palm Sunday broadcast upon which occasion he had said that the candidates for governor seemed to lack that necessary something that he defined as Christian leadership, and that if the folks thought O'Daniel himself should run to drop him a post card. O'Daniel's score on the response was 54,499 in favor of his running to four asking him not to run. Of the four, he explained, one was a crackpot, another a candidate himself, and the other two were both. The O'Daniel announcement followed.

None of the other candidates considered O'Daniel as anything except another man seeking state-wide publicity for the $100 filing fee. There were already twelve candidates in the field and Pappy O'Daniel, as he styled himself, was the thirteenth. Ernest still considered the jovial, rotund and popular attorney general as the man to beat. McCraw had his own fears about the redhead from Amarillo and no one else.

Soon there was talk that Allred was really prompting O'Daniel and had encouraged his appeal for post cards and the subsequent announcement. The Allred theory was said to be that O'Daniel would be an even match for McCraw; and that Thompson, the dignified, competent, and proven leader, could take over.

The fact is that Allred had probably taken exception to an ill-advised speech Thompson made in Sulphur Springs about two weeks before the O'Daniel announcement. The colonel had attacked de-liberalization of old-age pensions in an utterance that smacked of opportunism. He said that parents should not be denied pensions simply because "children were making a few dollars more than they actually needed for necessities." Allred, a great liberal and a staunch New Dealer, had proposed de-liberalization with the type of political courage one might attribute to a man of Thompson's character. His intention was to eliminate the chiselers so the needy might get the benefit of all available state funds. In fact, many had taken Allred's de-liberalization stand as his political swan song and a definite indication that he would not himself be a candidate, leaving the way clear to Thompson. In the same Sulphur Springs speech Thompson had accused the administration of bringing in out-of-state pension investigators. Sulphur Springs was probably where Allred parted company with Thompson and turned to O'Daniel, who had always been an Allred supporter. Time would prove that Thompson's speech and Allred's decision, based on that speech or not, were catastrophic to their respective authors.

By June, O'Daniel had begun to attract newspaper attention with his troop of hillbilly entertainers, an attractive wife, two handsome sons and a charming young daughter, as they made the rounds of the state. The hillbillies played and the children passed among the audience with miniature flour barrels into which the citizens would drop coins and bills of varying denominations. As he moved about the state his crowds began to grow, and the colonel looked upon him a bit nervously. In San Angelo, for instance, he drew 8000 to his talk, an unprecedented political audience for any place in West Texas. Then his Colorado City crowd of 3000 waited four hours to hear him when his sound truck broke down. Newspapers of the state were almost all behind either McCraw or Thompson, but they were spotlighting O'Daniel for his feature news value. Master showman that he was, O'Daniel made almost every move designed for publicity.

His platform was the Ten Commandments, hardly subject to attack by opponents. He was in favor of the

Golden Rule and against Johnson Grass and professional politicians. He was for more smokestacks and business-men and a $30 maximum pension for every soul over sixty-five years of age. O'Daniel claimed ignorance of politics, and his political palaver consisted of inspira-tional sermons on religion, patriotism, morals, thrift, and the home and family. The colonel planted a friend in his audience to ask the flour man how he was going to pay for the pensions. His answer was a typical O'Daniel classic.

"My friend," he said, "I'm glad you asked that ques-tion. Leon, strike up the band!"

There was no further answer and the crowd hooted and howled. Thompson was urging pension payments, taxes from natural resources and luxuries to pay for them, lower utility rates, and no other new taxes of any kind. He had platform planks calling for better schools and teachers' salaries, soil conservation, aid to labor and industrial development. McCraw had a similar platform except that he was even stronger for natural-resource taxes and the institution of a merit system for state employees. To the voters this was all old stuff they had heard before. O'Daniel was promising everything and asking nothing and he did it with music. He was soon sweeping the state.

McCraw, the master of repartee and the warm hand-shake, went on the air to attack O'Daniel.

"Can you imagine," he asked, "the immortal Jim Hogg standing on a wagon, wearing two-toned shoes, with perfume on the back of his ears, singing 'Jose-phine'?"

But the O'Daniel express rolled on. Leon, the guitar player, kept shouting for Pappy to pass the biscuits. The colonel and his erstwhile competitor for the governorship, McCraw, knew they were being bowled over. The evidence was never greater than it was the night the hillbilly flour salesman from Ohio by way of Kansas drew 35,000 people for his rally in the state capitol right under the noses of the "professional politicians." By this time most of the oilmen were on O'Daniel's bandwagon. They didn't want Ernest to win and give up his Commission seat, and they didn't want either Ernest or McCraw to win on a platform of higher natural-resources taxes. They didn't know about McCraw, but they did know that what the colonel promised in political platform he would carry out to the letter. The handwriting was scrawled all over the skies of Texas on the final night of the campaign.

When the votes were counted the colonel's gubernatorial doom was sealed in biscuit dough and dusted with flour. There was no second primary in the governor's race. O'Daniel had over 573,000 votes. The colonel was in second place with some 231,000 and McCraw was 80,000 votes behind that. Hunter ran a very poor fourth and the last nine candidates shared less than 40,000 votes among them.

Ernest Thompson's first political defeat was a bitter pill for him to swallow. Had he lost to Bill McCraw he might have been able to reconcile himself, but he considered O'Daniel a fake, a fraud and a political mountebank. One consolation was that he never learned how many of his oil friends were O'Daniel backers. The

strange thing about Pappy was that hardly anyone admitted having voted for him or supporting him but he
got all of the votes. If the colonel had needed any proof
that oilmen had supported the flour man he should have
recognized it in the pressure that O'Daniel yielded to
when he reappointed the colonel to the Interstate Oil
Compact Commission. But even that didn't change
Ernest's opinion and each passing day served to confirm
it more definitely.

The 1938 campaign brought the colonel a disappointment far more severe than that of losing the governorship, however. When all of the votes had been counted
Jerry Sadler, a young, roughshod, snuff-dipping East
Texas lawyer, had beaten Judge C. V. Terrell. This
had been the fulfillment of the prediction made by Tom
Foster, the Kilgore newspaperman, when the Sunday
shutdown order for East Texas was invoked. It was not
so much the shutdown that did it as it was Sadler's
side-show campaign which far outdid even the colorful
O'Daniel three-ring circus. The colonel's great regret,
though it was far too late, was that he had devoted his
time to an unnecessary race for governor when he should
have been helping the judge win. The truth was that
the colonel had no reason to believe that Terrell was in
the slightest danger of defeat. Sadler, however, was not
to embrace Lon Smith as a partner. He was smart
enough to hold himself out as an individual to settle the
issues between Thompson and Smith when they arose.
The result was that Texas now had a Commission composed of three men each with his own ideas. In little
things they differed, but in the big policy matters there

was almost no disagreement. There was a papal-like infallibility to the Commission's orders where the question of conservation was concerned. Sadler respected the genius in Thompson as well as the high esteem in which he was held by all segments of the industry.

The discovery and flush production of oil in Illinois even while the 1938 campaign was going on had brought new problems to the oil industry. Although Illinois was a participant in the Interstate Oil Compact, its laws were not sufficient to cope with the problem of more than a quarter of a million barrels of oil daily. Productionwise, this was almost another East Texas. Soon the market was flooded again and the problem of controls became more acute. In Texas there was a hue and cry for the curtailment of drilling.

At the very height of the political campaigns of both the colonel and the judge, it had actually become necessary to add Saturday shutdowns in East Texas to the already long established Sunday shutdowns. Both Terrell and Thompson had joined in promulgating this order in spite of its almost fatal political implications. At that point John Schroeder of the East Texas Independent Petroleum Association had sounded a new call for federal control. He contended that both state control and the oil-states compact had failed to stop profligate waste in Illinois and a flood of oil on the market. At a meeting in Gladewater a petition was offered urging Governor Allred to call the legislature into special session for the express purpose of instituting impeachment proceedings against the three members of the Railroad Commission.

With the election over things got little better. Illinois

oil was still gurgling out of the wellheads with un-diminished flow. For a fleeting moment, even the strong-est of states rights' advocates seemed to lose confidence in the ability of the states to control their own affairs. Ickes was in high glee in Washington.

At the December statewide hearing, almost every witness urged curtailment of drilling. Thompson re-minded them there was nothing in the law that would permit such a program even if he favored it. Stanley Gill, a Houston engineer, was quoted by the Associated Press as saying that wildcatting should be discouraged instead of being encouraged. The Bureau of Mines forecasts of market demand actually amounted to a top allowable for co-operating states. Now the operators urged the Com-mission to set top allowables for fields. That, they con-tended, would put a halt to development wells being drilled for the present in proven fields.

Lon Smith, late in 1938, attacked the Saturday and Sunday shutdown rules for East Texas, but the operators were doing little complaining other than that they wanted the rule extended to the remainder of the state. One of East Texas' most fabulous characters, F. W. Fisher, politician and country lawyer known affection-ately in the industry as "Big Fish," said that if the purpose of the shutdowns was to prevent waste and sta-bilize prices that he felt that his part of the country was being selfish and that the same benefits should be shared with the rest of the states. A state senator from Dallas called the curtailments price-fixing. Jack Blalock, an old Thompson crony in the federal-control fight, contended that further curtailment would cost Texas many valuable markets. The president of the Independent Petroleum Association of America, Charles Roeser, said that if the week-end shutdowns were extended to the entire state there would be 10,000 exceptions since many small towns depended on oil wells for their natural gas.

The industry was still in the infancy of a program of stabilization. It had not matured. It was still a question of whose ox was being gored. The colonel demonstrated his patience in listening to all, weighing the facts, and then making a decision. His method of finding facts was to put experts in the field to dig them out. At the December meeting in the Stephen F. Austin Hotel in the capital city he asked V. E. Cottingham, the chief engineer of the Commission, for his opinion of the situation. The engineer's recommendation was more nearly that of the "Big Fish" than any of the others.

The shutdowns were extended to the entire State with the necessary exceptions to provide a flow of natural gas for cities that depended on casing-head gas from oil wells.

The fact that it was the last state-wide meeting in which Judge Terrell would take part gave the December hearing an unusual significance. The colonel mentioned the fact and expressed his great regret at the departure of the man who had taken his father's place. He closed the meeting by recounting the good man's many contributions to the vast program of conservation and by reminding those present of their obligations to the judge. The meeting ended with a loud but dignified standing ovation for the quiet man of unchallenged integrity and ability whom the people had denied another term on the Commission that he considered a part of his life.

CHAPTER XII

No Nickel for Grandma

The Texas legislature came and went in 1939 without doing a thing about the pensions Governor O'Daniel had promised the voters. He had mentioned a natural-resources tax in his message, but he put more emphasis on what he called a transactions tax. Actually it was the sales tax he had campaigned against under another name. He did nothing about abolishing the poll tax and very little about the Ten Commandments.

As he watched these things happening, the colonel concluded that the people who had overwhelmingly elected Pappy, the Biscuit Passer, must certainly regret their action already. Everywhere he went he heard that O'Daniel was a mistake. The old folks were disappointed. They were far worse off than they had been while Allred was governor.

With all of this turning over in his mind it didn't take Ernest Thompson long to decide that he would again run against the flour merchant in 1940. Frequently the colonel wrote letters to the governor with copies for the press, complaining about something. Such an incident happened in early August of 1939.

The colonel was on active duty with his regiment in Camp Hulen. He had been transferred from the infantry to the quartermaster corps in 1931 and four years later had organized the 111th Quartermaster Regiment and had become its proud commanding officer. That was when he was promoted to full colonel. In 1939 the colonel was more convinced than ever that there would be war in Europe and that this country would eventually be pulled into it. His interest in the National Guard was that of a man who believed it was his patriotic duty, as a trained soldier, to stand ready to serve his country. He had a firm belief that the only possible way the United States could avoid war was by being militarily as well as economically strong enough to demand respect in Europe and in Asia. He had constantly deplored the sending of petroleum to Japan and had actually prohibited it in so far as he was able in Texas. Furthermore, he had attempted to ascertain that Texas oil sent to Europe was sent for peaceful purposes and under no circumstances to the war machines of the Fascist Italians or the Nazi Germans.

Ernest Thompson's summer training was rudely interrupted with an announcement in the *Houston Post* on the morning of August 10. Harry F. Sinclair, the "Lone Wolf" of the integrated oil-company magnates, arbitrarily reduced the Sinclair-Prairie Oil Marketing Company's crude-oil prices in the mid-continent area, effective immediately. The announcement surprised the oil world but few executives believed anyone would follow Sinclair's example any more than they had followed an earlier one-cent a gallon gasoline raise he had tried. He had been forced to cut back on the price of gasoline and the crude price reduction followed.

Two days later the entire oil industry was stunned when Humble Oil and Refining Company announced a reduction in prices ranging from five cents to thirty-two cents a barrel, according to gravity and grade. Humble's explanation was that competitors were purchasing oil for less in the field and that they were forced to meet the price. The cause of the trouble, generally, was the wide open and uncontrolled flow of oil in Illinois where there was no semblance of conservation.

With these events Colonel Thompson sent a telegram to Governor O'Daniel urging a special session of the legislature to pass a five-cent-a-barrel oil tax for old age pensions. He said that if oil prices could be cut an average of twenty cents a barrel at a time when crude in storage was at a twelve-year low and demand was at its all-time high, there was no reason why a nickel a barrel for the old folks was an unreasonable demand. He said it would bring in $75,000 a day, ample to pay pensions in full currently—plus a tremendous reserve for the future even if the state should run out of oil. The colonel told the governor that the oil price-cut could cost Texas $100 million a year and that the Railroad Commission would immediately take whatever action it deemed possible to remove the cause of the action, whether it be overproduction or something else.

O'Daniel replied to the colonel's letter promptly, with copies to the press. The reply was forceful but cold. It was addressed to "E. O. Thompson, Palacios, Texas." The governor said he had no intention of calling the legislature which had already been in Austin for 163 days at a cost of $850,000 to the taxpayers that year and done nothing. He didn't think the lawmakers would do anything in another thirty days. O'Daniel suggested that Thompson return to Austin and do something within the scope of existing laws about the oil situation. That, the governor said, was Thompson's responsibility. And he said that the colonel might be able to do something through the Interstate Oil Compact Commission, "to which I appointed you." His closing line was that the only people wanting a special session were a few "professional politicians" who were anxious to mend their political fences. The colonel burned and sizzled in his torrid seaside barracks on the Gulf.

Thompson obtained a leave of absence and returned to Austin where he prepared an order to shut down all oil fields in the state of Texas for thirty days. The basis of the order was waste due to overproduction. Specifically, the order provided that the shutdown would enable the Commission to study conditions of above-ground storage including waste of crude oil by evaporation, to make overdue bottom hole pressure tests in all fields, and to inspect all wells with a view toward eliminating dead wells that might be carried on certain books merely to get production allowables.

Smith and Sadler were out of pocket for the time. The colonel finally found Sadler in Houston and went to him with the order. He waited until Smith, who was in Galveston, could be found. Finally the order was signed for fifteen days instead of thirty and became effective on August 15 at 7 A.M. It closed 87,000 oil wells.

The colonel, as the chairman, called an emergency meeting of the Interstate Oil Compact Commission in

Oklahoma City for the morning of the 15th. Representatives of Louisiana, Arkansas, Kansas and New Mexico met in Governor Leon Phillips' office. It was brief.

"I have called this meeting solely to tell you what Texas has done," Thompson said. "If there is too much oil above ground, as we have been told, we in Texas have acted to prevent actual physical waste. We took action in Texas exactly three hours ago. This price cut could force 100,000 marginal wells out of operation and result in the loss of millions of barrels of oil, the total loss of an irreplaceable resource."

That was the extent of his message. The colonel then adjourned the meeting and returned directly to Austin. That day Oklahoma and New Mexico followed Texas' example. Arkansas and Kansas followed the next day. With that action 145,200 oil wells had been closed, slightly more than half of the wells in the United States. On August 19 Governor Earl Long of Louisiana told the press his state would shut down its wells for ten days. California and Illinois, both without conservation laws, and the other two major oil states, did nothing.

Back in Texas a majority of the independents and many of the majors approved of the action. The Texas Company, the Sun Oil Company, Gulf, and at first, Shell, refused to meet the Humble prices, but there was little crude to buy or sell anyway.

Throughout the vast Southwest and mid-continent areas newspaper headlines featured the Russian-German trade agreement and their nonaggression pact with the historic oil shutdown.

Thompson told the press that if the state regulatory

bodies, co-operating with the industry, could not be successful in preventing actual physical waste by reducing above-ground storage that the next step might be federal control. His old Compact-composing crony, Elwood Fouts, said in Houston that the price reductions plus the shutdown orders constituted a strong invitation to federal control. Sadler said that "Old Ickes is sitting up in Washington with an itching palm waiting to get his hands on the oil industry."

W. S. Farish of Standard Oil of New Jersey, himself one of the founders of the Humble Oil and Refining Company, explained the price cuts by saying that products stocks, especially gasoline, had been high for some time and were burdensome. He was answering a letter to the North Texas Oil and Gas Association. In the same reply he said that there was a need for stronger and better conservation laws, apparently referring to the wild orgy of production in Illinois and Louisiana.

Harry C. Wiess, president of Humble, in an advertisement in Texas newspapers, explained his company's action. He said that on the morning of Humble's cut more than 668,000 barrels of oil daily was available to competitors at prices below those Humble was paying. That, of course, included 150,000 barrels that Sinclair-Prairie was taking. He blamed "the flood of oil from Illinois and Louisiana, most of which is being produced wastefully in violation of conservation principles" as the primary responsibility, and said that the price of oil brought about by the competitive conditions was lower than should be realized.

Lon Smith told the press that the company might

have cut prices to fill up storage and then take an in-
ventory gain. He said it was an old trick.

Mr. Wiess's statement answered that, too. It said that
Humble worked on stocks only slightly in excess of the
amount its refineries required to avoid above-ground
storage as much as possible. He said his company did not
speculate in oil and did not desire to purchase oil at any
price to accumulate for storage.

At an emergency meeting, shortly before the fifteen
day shutdown period ended, Mr. Wiess told Colonel
Thompson that unless crude was made available his
company would be out within forty-eight hours. The
Commission decided to continue the shutdown, however,
and the other states did the same. Humble announced
that it was rescinding its price cut, effective the day of the
reduction. Thompson, nevertheless, signed the order for
a continuation of the shutdown. Smith and Sadler refused to sign, however, and the fields were reopened.

Had the price cuts obtained, there is little doubt that
thousands of marginal wells would have closed down as
the colonel claimed. Oil was selling at that time for
slightly more than $1 a barrel average. The reductions
amounted to about twenty percent of that. There was no
marginal well subsidy at that time and few of the wells
pumping from one to five barrels a day could have
survived without serious loss. The real "villains" were
Illinois with no conservation whatsoever, and Louisiana
with a law that was being abused by politicians who soon
afterward paid the penalty of corruption.

Humble had been forced into an untenable position.
It was one that might have brought back many of the

miseries of the preconservation days had it not been for the immediate and effective action of the redhead from Amarillo.

The shutdown did an unusual amount of good. East Texas pressure picked up forty-eight pounds, and other fields reported much better flowing conditions in many instances. During the shutdown engineers checked hundreds of wells. Many dead wells that were getting their allowables from flowing wells on the same leases were eliminated from the schedules. Run-down wells and fields were put in good working order. No workers were laid off. Both the majors and the independents co-operated.

But above all, another threat of federal control was stopped. When the shouting was over the state regulatory bodies were in the best position they had ever been. All doubt about the colonel's willingness to act in an emergency had vanished. The oil companies had a new respect for the man and his determination. His order had been based on sound physical waste prevention.

The battle of the big shutdown had hardly settled when Hitler marched into Poland on September 1. Two days later England and France declared war on Germany. Overnight the oil situation changed. The war was slow in the early days. Some called it a war that was not a war. But the pressure was building up all of the time.

On September 21 the colonel wrote a letter to his friend in the White House. He explained the reasons for the recent shutdown and then said that another problem faced the industry. He told President Roosevelt that he feared a frenzy of war demand for petroleum might cause some states to overproduce. He asked the President to assure the states that the Bureau of Mines estimates would continue to be accurate. He said the Bureau had done an excellent job but that he believed some of the oil states needed a word from the President on the subject. In closing, the colonel said that he thought the nation should know, through the President, that the states could supply oil for any emergency and that there was no cause for alarm on that score.

With the passing months the bitterness between O'Daniel and the colonel continued to increase. The governor's frequent references to "professional politicians" rankled. Thompson told a group of clubwomen in Dallas that he was proud to be a politician approaching his craft with a professional experience. He said he would never consider entering the flour business without knowing something about it.

O'Daniel had failed in almost every campaign pledge. He had fallen down badly in co-operating with the federal government in an air defense plan. He ignored a request by patriotic groups to investigate subversive activities within the state. Thompson accused O'Daniel of doing nothing in the way of preparedness for the state. O'Daniel blamed the professional politicians.

By early February Thompson had come to the conclusion that anyone could beat O'Daniel. Never before in the history of Texas, in the colonel's opinion, had such a misfit happened to the people of the state as this man from Kansas.

The colonel's advisers, however, were even worse in his second campaign than they were in the first. His five-cent oil tax suggested from Camp Hulen in 1939 became a keystone of his platform. He started a state-wide chant for "a nickel for grandma." He became vitriolic in his tirades against the governor and shouted abusive epithets in his direction.

By the time all of the announcements were in, Thompson's campaign was well under way. The most surprising announcement to the colonel was that of his new colleague on the Commission, Jerry Sadler. Harry Hines, former chairman of the state highway commission, was another candidate. A fourth was Ma Ferguson, back for her last fling in the political arena.

The colonel went his merry way, however, ignoring all except the man in the mansion. He took advantage of the war fever and O'Daniel's lack of a service record. All over the state, when he came to that part of his speeches he shouted loudly into microphones, "Where were you, Wilbert?" after telling what the other male candidates had done in the way of war participation. Thompson claimed that while others were fighting in 1918, O'Daniel had stayed home in Kansas to sell flour in a patriotic red, white and blue painted automobile. Thompson got into little things and beat himself with a wild frenzy of mudslinging, completely out of character. His speech writers wrote as if they had been working for O'Daniel.

O'Daniel ignored the charges and even took advantage of the personal abuse by stating that he regretted that his wife and children had to stand the humiliation of hearing professional politicians lambaste him from one side of the state to the other. He kept talking and singing and promising and taking up nickels and dimes and quarters in little wooden barrels. He toured the state in a new $15,000 sound truck that Thompson pointed out was a gift, the size of which alone exceeded the legal limit of campaign contributions. O'Daniel said the truck was a personal automobile. Thompson accused some big oil companies and many of the wealthy independents of backing O'Daniel.

The campaign was almost degrading to the colonel. He left his dignity at home; and it is possible that dignity might have paid off this time against a political campaign of clowning and fiddle-playing.

But when it was all over the result was worse for the colonel than before. O'Daniel had 645,000 votes and Thompson again had the consolation prize with 257,000. Hines, Ferguson and Sadler ran in that order. There was no run-off. The governor had fifty-four percent of the total vote.

The colonel learned a bitter lesson. He learned that he could not compete with a political phenomenon. No one has yet figured out what made O'Daniel tick. The people kept quiet and voted for the man. There were no great O'Daniel organizations or rallies, except when he was present himself. He made great use of the radio. But in Austin, and later in Washington, he accomplished little. It was unfortunate that Thompson who had set the mansion in Austin as his goal early in life had to come along just at the moment of a man like O'Daniel. Possibly if he hadn't attacked de-liberalization of pensions back in

1937 there might have been no pressure on O'Daniel
from Allred to run, and Thompson might have defeated
McCraw. Those thoughts haunted the colonel, but when
he was through with them he was through with trying
to be governor. He decided that fate had meant him to
be where he was, on the Railroad Commission. The oilmen, many of whom helped O'Daniel merely to assure
Thompson's remaining on the Railroad Commission,
were happy when he let it be known that he was no
longer interested in the governorship.

The 1939 gubernatorial campaign overshadowed
another race that was to prove equally important. Lon
Smith had decided not to seek re-election because of ill
health. Olin Culberson, Thompson's appointee and
champion of many a gas-rate case along with the colonel
had been fired in the summer of 1939 by Sadler and
Smith. In the 1940 election he had announced and won
the Smith seat on the Commission after a bitter battle
with a half-dozen excellent opponents.

That election was a satisfaction to the colonel because
he had a great admiration for Culberson. He knew that
he was able and honest and would add experience and
stature to the Commission just at a time when his service
would probably be needed most.

CHAPTER XIII

No Plane Failed to Fly

The nightmare of the colonel's two political campaigns against a foe who never met defeat at the Texas polls was over. Ernest Thompson was glad. He was resigned to not being elected governor of Texas but he was puzzled at the reaction of the people to a man who promised so much and gave so little. The second loss to O'Daniel left the colonel slightly stunned and somewhat humiliated. For the first time in his life he had lost his temper and his balance in public. O'Daniel was the most frustrating man any candidate ever had to face. He generalized on everything, answering with music from his hillbillies in reply to all specific questions, showed up frequently and unexpectedly at church services over the state, or preached sermons over the radio on paid political time. The colonel's friends in industry, labor organizations, farmers and businessmen, all of whom were obligated to him for his accomplishments, plus the thousands of Texas veterans who idolized him, gave him an organization that should have spelled political victory for any man. O'Daniel, on the other hand, had nothing. Not many people would admit they were even going to vote for him. Yet his defeat of Thompson,

Hines and Ferguson, all great names in Texas politics, was total.

The colonel wanted to forget it all. His gubernatorial ambitions were completely throttled. Events to come in the next fifteen years would prove the wisdom of fate in leaving this servant of the people where he could do the most good. O'Daniel might have been a blessing. Thompson probably could have defeated anyone else for governor. But, by becoming governor, he would have been removed from the one office wherein he could best serve his state and nation.

It wasn't too long after the 1940 elections were over that the colonel's unit, the 111th Quartermaster Regiment, was ordered to active duty with the 36th Division at Camp Bowie near Brownwood, about 140 miles from Austin. The war clouds were growing darker daily. The colonel made arrangements to train his regiment for war and at the same time be available for important conferences with his colleagues in the capital. Camp Bowie and the camaradarie of his men was a good place to escape the memories of two disastrous campaigns.

Within a few months the colonel's regiment was one of the best trained in the army. He was a good commander with a flair for discipline and for the maintenance of excellent troop morale. He was always proud of the fact that his soldiers were largely college graduates and that many of the enlisted men were well qualified to become officers in the event of an emergency. And the colonel had no doubt that the emergency would come.

Hitler and Mussolini were bearing down in Europe

and the Japanese were moving steadily forward in the Orient. Russia had joined forces with the Germans and it was apparent to a man of clear vision, such as Ernest Thompson, that events were leading directly to a war between totalitarianism and democracy.

In July of 1941, Colonel Thompson was returned to the line as commander of the 141st Infantry. In his farewell to his QM regiment he pointed out that the men had compiled a safety record unexcelled in the army. His motorized units usually ended their trips with a report that bore the tagline "without incident or accident."

As much as he regretted leaving the quartermaster unit he had organized, trained and commanded, the colonel felt happy back with his doughboys. He was a popular leader from the beginning. He taught his men how to fight and he taught them the value of spit and polish. Before he had been in the unit a month he had authorized a new and snappy salute that gained for the regiment the nickname of the "Stargazers." On the famous Louisiana maneuvers his antitank company knocked out nineteen of twenty "enemy" tanks to establish a record. His regiment marched twenty-seven miles in thirty hours, with only ten of the 2000 troops dropping out. It was a conditioned and a war-ready unit. Many of his reforms in training were adopted by the national army and it was believed that, should war come, he would immediately become one of the highest-ranking combat commanders.

President Roosevelt had another idea for the colonel, however. He realized the nation's proximity to war and the essentiality of oil to war. In this connection the President recognized that Texas oil production would be the key to petroleum for defense, and that Thompson's leadership was far more vital in that respect than it was in the army field forces. Harold Ickes had already become co-ordinator for petroleum. Thompson, whose state would be vital to the nation's petroleum program, had pledged complete co-operation to his old enemy.

On November 22, 1941, barely two weeks before the Japanese attack on Pearl Harbor and America's entry into World War II, the colonel was relieved from active duty to return to his position in Austin. The 111th Quartermaster regiment and the 141st Infantry staged a review for his benefit. Thousands of young men, who were soon to be among the first available combat troops, paid high respect to their old commander. The 141st Infantry was actually one of the crack units of the citizen army.

At noon the officers of the two regiments gave a banquet for their colonel. He was called the "finest soldier of the division," an accolade he cherished far more than anything else that could have been said of him. When the speeches were over he was asked to say a few words. His only reply was, "There's nothing I can say." He was choked with emotion and regret at leaving these fine men with whom he felt so much at ease. The officers, including General Fred Walker, the division commander; General Eugene Eversberg, brigade commander, and his successor, Lt. Col. Miller Ainsworth, sang "Auld Lang Syne" and Ernest nudged May and asked her to lend her golden voice to the virile chorus.

"But I don't know the words," May admitted to her astonished husband.

Fifteen mess sergeants presented their colonel with fifteen pairs of autographed white gloves as a remembrance of the fact that he always wore them when inspecting the mess. A framed scroll, signed personally by the 2700 officers and men of the 141st, was also presented to him to become one of his proudest possessions.

During the past year the colonel had not had much co-operation from his colleagues Sadler and Culberson. The two men had placed Ernest in a minority position for the first time since he had come on the Commission. It was ironic that this should happen with the election of Culberson whom the colonel had appointed to the Commission in 1932 as one of his first official acts. Culberson and Thompson, through the years, had been close. Frequently Thompson depended on Culberson's good judgment, particularly in gas-rate cases.

Minority though he may have been, the red head from Amarillo had not lost his sharpness as a fighter. When he couldn't get his colleagues to hear him he took his battles to the people.

In May he told the West Texas Chamber of Commerce that Hitler had ample oil. This was contrary to some public thinking at the time. And the colonel warned that if the Germans took Iran and Iraq they would have all of the petroleum they would ever need. He cheered his audience, however, by revealing that the United States had half of the known oil reserves, and that Texas, "simply by taking off the nine shutdown days now in effect could supply a five-million-man army, a 50,000 plane group constantly in the air, and a vast two-ocean navy," all with no civilian curtailment. The colonel blasted defense strikes and pointed to a tragic lack of supplies. He told how 36th Division troops had been forced to use firecrackers in order to make training beneficially realistic on maneuvers because of a shortage of guns and ammunition while defense plants were being picketed.

At the October state-wide hearing the colonel had called for all possible production without physical waste in view of the national emergency. Sadler replied that the state was already producing 75,000 barrels a day over the Bureau of Mine's estimates and added that if any operator expected to get his allowables raised he should go to the chairman [Thompson] because "I am not interested." Culberson said he believed the commission should stick to the present yardstick, meaning the estimate.

In November, shortly before he was relieved of his military duties, the colonel appeared before the American Association of Oil-Well Drilling Contractors and described stocks as shockingly low in view of the world situation. The United States had a sixty-day supply of crude in storage and a forty-five-day supply of gasoline. Hitler, on the other hand, he said, had a minimum supply of a year's petroleum products. Thompson said that anticipated demand by the military with a schedule of 100,000 planes, 125,000 tanks and 280,000 motor vehicles for the next five years was overwhelming. He said that soon almost five million barrels of oil would be needed daily in America and that at present there were 200 million barrels of empty storage space that should be filled immediately. That speech was less than three weeks before Pearl Harbor. He alone, however, could not authorize allowables to fill the empty storage.

Since the days of the beginning of strict proration the colonel had sought to encourage wildcatters. Even when others were talking about overproduction he was trying to find a way to increase new reserves. One of his ideas was a discovery allowable that would permit a wildcatter to recover a large part of his investment in a short time. It took the war and the great fear of enormous demands for him to get his point over. At the January, 1942, state-wide proration hearing Sadler and Culberson agreed to a policy of discovery allowables. The commission set a schedule ranging from forty barrels daily for wells up to 1000 feet deep to 480 barrels a day for wells up to 11,000 feet for the first six months of wildcat production, or until more than five wells had been drilled in a new field.

The war quickly brought a serious shortage of transportation. German submarines started sinking tankers in the Gulf of Mexico and it was almost impossible to move oil from Gulf ports by water, the normal mode of transportation for petroleum. This forced eighteen days of shutdowns for Texas fields. This condition caused hundreds of independent oilmen to face bankruptcy. Senator Tom Connally of Texas proposed a bill providing for federal loans to independents who were in financial trouble. Thompson backed the bill and suggested that the money be loaned on negotiable script for the value of oil not produced during shutdown days. Banks could accept the script on loans payable when it was possible to produce the shutin oil. Independent oilmen rejected the idea of personal financial aid by the government and Thompson dropped his support for the bill on the grounds that the situation was not as bad as he had thought.

The colonel took a dim view of proposed gasoline rationing in Texas, contending that it would hinder rather than help the war effort. Rationing was already in effect on the east coast in May, and Ernest Thompson pointed out that for the first time in history, government was restricting production of oil in one part of the country and rationing gasoline in another part. He urged slow driving and extreme care of automobiles and tires, "because there are not going to be any more for some time to come."

The building of the Big Inch pipeline, capable of carrying 300,000 barrels of crude daily from Texas to the coast, was authorized in June. This was an idea that Thompson had advanced several years earlier only to run into opposition from other transportation interests.

Another election year for the colonel had rolled around by 1942 but he hardly had time to do any more than make a formal announcement for re-election. There were few speeches and very little campaign literature in spite of the fact that Lester Boone, a state representative from Pampa, ran against him. In the first primary the colonel received 572,828 votes which was almost 325,000 more than Boone, his nearest competitor who had less than 250,000 votes. A third candidate hardly made a ripple at the polls with a scant 70,000 out of a total of almost 900,000 votes cast.

The war brought the big payoff for Texas' good conservation years under Thompson. His policy of promoting the finding of more oil while holding production down to the most efficient rate of recovery was reaping a rich dividend. As other states strained to make the quotas set for them by Ickes, Thompson's Texas responded generously to every demand made on it, including making up the shortages for other states. Illinois, for instance, where oil reservoirs were virtually destroyed in a wild orgy of greedy and uncontrolled drilling and over-production, had reached its peak production of 462,000 barrels a day in the month before Pearl Harbor. When the oil was needed by the nation for defense, Illinois production was rapidly and steadily declining until by the end of the war the state was producing barely 200,000 barrels of crude a day and that with tremendous effort.

By July of 1942 Texas had celebrated the bringing in of its 100,000th producing oil well. The state was producing 1,400,000 barrels of oil daily on a twenty-two-day schedule which was enough to provide forty percent of the total United States production. The other eight days were available on call. At that time Thompson's state had fifty-seven percent of the nation's known oil reserves. He and his colleagues had done their job well, and there were few who would deny that the steadying influence had been the colonel. In fact, other states were able to do their part in some instances because they, too, had heeded the colonel's wise counsel.

August brought a new member to the Commission. Beauford Jester, himself an oilman, was appointed to the

Commission by Governor Coke Stevenson when Sadler voluntarily went into the army.

Thompson was alarmed, late in 1942, when Commission engineers reported that the flow of salt water in the East Texas wells was increasing and that the reservoir pressure was being dissipated rapidly by the new development. On November 19 an order was issued limiting the net production of water to ten barrels to a barrel of oil. Net water was that not returned to the strata from which the oil was being produced. Provision was made for shutting off water-producing wells, with allowables for such wells to be produced from non-water wells. Culberson believed the order was contrary to the marginal well law, and dissented. Thompson argued that it was most important to maintain the pressure of the giant reservoir. Several major companies and a number of independents joined together in 1942 to form a salt-water injection company and reinject 120,000 barrels of water daily on the west side of the field, the direction from which the water-drive came. Thompson had taken an early interest in experiments being made, even before salt water showed up, by the pioneers of this company. He had lent his encouragement as he always did on matters of technical advancement within the industry, and through his influence the Commission allowed an extra barrel of oil for every fifty barrels of salt water successfully reinjected. Due largely to the new salt water injection program, it was possible to cut the water-oil ratio to five-to-one in August of 1943 and at the same time meet the Petroleum Administration for War quota for the field. Later in the year a

184

court in Austin upheld the water order, ruling that it was not in conflict with the marginal well law. By 1944 the program had worked so well that eighty percent of the salt water produced in East Texas was being returned to the producing sands and the bottom hole pressure in the field had started a healthy rise. The colonel had again protected and saved his old friend, the Black Giant.

The OPA had placed a ceiling of $1.20 on crude oil in 1942 and by the middle of the year Thompson was urging Washington to raise the ceiling by twenty-five cents, to stimulate independents into searching for oil. He also warned that the stripper-wells' three-billion barrels of reserves would have to be abandoned by operators who could not afford to continue operating at a loss. The price relief never came during the war, in spite of Ickes' pledged aid to Thompson. The colonel subordinated all of his ill feelings toward Ickes during the war and frequently reminded the oil leaders that he considered wartime oil orders from Ickes as directives from the commander-in-chief. The PAW chief and his agents frequently found fault with and held up oil produced in excess of government certificates in the face of Thompson's urgent and constant pleas to stockpile oil in unused storage.

By 1943 the Big Inch pipeline was completed as far as Illinois, and oil went east from there by rail. Fabulous Burt Hull and a staff of indomitable pipeliners were doing a superhuman job in the emergency. The Little Inch had been authorized by then and there was some talk of having it start at Chicago instead of Houston and Beaumont. Thompson said the logistics of such a proposal were absurd—that the pipeline should start at the source of supply. He pointed out further that the government could recover its investment from the line if it were started in Texas by converting both the Big and Little Inch lines to gas carriers after the war and selling them.

By mid-1943 Texas was producing almost two million barrels of war oil daily, the highest production of any state up to that time. The price freeze continued to irritate the colonel. He knew that more reserves were vital and that it was impossible for independents, the most important oil finders, to risk money when there was little chance of recovery, even if they hit oil. But Washington continued to turn a deaf ear. Drilling was deeper, labor was more expensive, supplies and equipment were almost twice their prewar prices, but still the price of crude oil continued pegged. In addition to all of this some PAW field agents were making themselves obnoxious by their lack of knowledge of oil production and their insistence on silly regulations. The patience of oilmen frequently approached the breaking point, but always the sage advice of the colonel and his appeal to their patriotism helped keep them going ahead in spite of PAW stupidities and OPA price restrictions that had nothing to do with conservation or the development of needed reserves. In 1943, for instance, the PAW was permitting refineries to operate at only seventy-eight percent of capacity, with gasoline stortages everywhere except in Texas.

The colonel attempted to impress upon Washington the seriousness of the situation. Drilling costs were up forty percent. Only 307 wildcats were drilled in Texas in the first five months of 1943 and of those, all except twenty-three were dry. Thompson's urgent appeal for price increases to stimulate drilling resulted in nothing except a complete refusal by Economic Stabilizer Fred Vinson. He suggested a system of government subsidies as a solution to the problem. Thompson replied to Vinson that no one in the oil business wanted subsidies for flush production but said that something would have to be done about marginal wells. It was mid-1944 before stripper-well subsidies were authorized by the government, and then Thompson expressed his thanks for helping the little pumpers but said this was still no answer to the problem of finding new discoveries which were vital since even Texas was about to reach its own limits under the strain of tremendous demand without benefit of necessary new reserves. Washington could not understand.

The colonel haunted the national capitol, fighting for the best interests of oil. In spite of their differences, he continued to work with Ickes to obtain the best results. He was constantly careful, however, to guard against any policy that might tend to leave Ickes in charge of oil after the war, or anything that he was certain from his experience would be detrimental to the industry as a whole. He took as much interest in other states' problems as he did in those of Texas. Oil editors over the country were impressed with the magnificent job the colonel was doing for the country as well as the industry. His understanding of the problems, plus his ability to state those problems in a concise and fresh manner, readily understandable to all who heard him was a remarkable aid. Claude Barrow, the oil editor of the *Daily Oklahoman*, suggested in 1944 that the colonel be made a one-man public-relations counsel for the industry. He said the colonel had a nose for news and what elements made news, plus the fact that "he knows the industry and could represent it at all levels. And he is a fighter who does not give up," Barrow added.

By early 1944 the colonel had about all of the PAW he could stand. As a member of the National Conference of Petroleum Regulatory Authorities, a group of some seventy-five experts, appointed to advise Secretary Ickes, Thompson urged the end of PAW.

"We have met and met and met and now we have, at last, an opportunity to justify our meetings. We can announce to the Administrator of the PAW that we can handle the oil-well spacing, drilling and producing problems within our sovereign states," the colonel said.

He then pointed out that without the PAW, operators could be saved precious hours of filling out forms and traveling to and from Washington, that skilled men on the PAW staff could be released back to the industry where they were urgently needed, that the duplication of duties by both PAW and state regulatory bodies could be eliminated, that there was ample production (Texas was producing only twenty-three days a month and was capable of full production when and if needed) and that the elimination of red tape would result in more exploration.

"We might as well get right down to pay dirt and state

that we are fearful that the federal government is attempting to set up a super-duper oil and gas conservation and production regulatory bureau under the guise of War Emergency that will not liquidate itself when the emergency is over," he said in conclusion.

A few days later Ralph K. Davies, an executive of the Standard Oil Company of California, and Ickes' deputy administrator, answered Thompson by stating that the PAW believed a need for regulations continued because of material shortages and to make sure that the few wells drilled in 1944 would result in a maximum of sustained productive capacity for the materials and manpower expended. He added that he too, however, looked forward to the day when the PAW would be no longer needed.

The colonel replied a few days later, pointing out that the government had allocated enough steel for a 1200-mile pipeline in Arabia which would not be completed for two years, and at the same time had limited well completions in the United States to 24,000, many less than the industry had hoped to drill to be able to meet the tremendous war demand and find new reserves. A month later the Interstate Oil Compact Commission adopted a Thompson-sponsored resolution calling for the abandonment of the PAW's drilling, spacing and production activities but retaining regulations dealing with War Production Board requirements regarding the allocation of critical materials.

The battle between the colonel and red tape went on until October 24, 1945 when the PAW gave its final report to the Petroleum Industry War Council. In August the colonel had hailed the end of gasoline rationing by saying "Fill 'er up should be the joy cry of the nation." He had never been convinced that rationing had ever been absolutely necessary.

Ickes himself had said in a speech to Wisconsin oilmen earlier in the war, "This is a war of machines and of ships and of airplanes powered by oil. In short this is an oil war. The side which, by interrupting the flow of petroleum products to the enemy, and which, at the same time, can supply its own tanks, its mechanized guns, its fighting ships and its airplanes with gasoline, lubricants and fuel oils of the proper kind, at the time required, and in the right places, is the side which will eventually win this world-wide conflict."

Besides fuel and lubrication for mechanized armies, the oil industry had supplied other important items of warfare including asphalt for roads and landing strips, toluene for TNT, butadiene for synthetic rubber, jellied gasoline for flame throwers and incendiary bombs, smoke for smoke screens, and even wax and grease for packaging everything from guns to rations.

Rommel's famed *Afrika Korps* fell for a lack of fuel for its mechanical monsters. The *Luftwaffe* and Hitler's *Panzer* divisions stalled for a lack of gasoline and became useless heaps of steel on roads and runways. Oil had won the war, and lack of it had lost it. The colonel proudly pointed to the fact that Texas' conservation program, prudently, diligently and efficiently pursued, had been able to supply eighty percent of the oil necessary for United States and all Allied forces. The loss of the Black

Giant could have easily meant the loss of the freedom to the entire world. The redhead from Amarillo was justly proud of his part in preserving that great reservoir and in working out the lessons that were applied in many other oil fields.

The war role the colonel welcomed the most was his mission to Europe in early 1945. He was ordered back into uniform for a special assignment to follow gasoline and oil from the ports to the front and suggest to the War Department possible methods of improving petroleum logistics.

In issuing the orders Undersecretary of War Bob Patterson had "ordered" the colonel to visit the 111th Quartermaster and the 141st Infantry regiments. "I know you will anyway," Patterson had said, "so I'll order you to do so and you won't come up AWOL." The colonel did and the regiments were inspired by his appearance. On April 15, the second anniversary of the 36th Division's landing at Oran, he was with the division at the front. Major General John Dallquist, division commander, presented him with a German 36th Division plaque for the Texas State Museum. The emblem had been captured by the colonel's old outfit a few days before. At the front the colonel visited with many old friends including Colonel E. E. Fogelson, Dallas oilman; Major Dawson Duncan, formerly of the *Dallas News* and one of his old capitol pressroom cronies; Lt. Col. Ray Lynch of the Railroad Commission staff in Austin; and even his antagonist of the 1936 campaign, Colonel Freeman Burford whose opposition had long since been forgotten and forgiven. The colonel made a complete survey of oil production in Arabia, Iraq, Iran, Kuwait and Bahrein on this trip.

After Colonel Thompson had reported to Patterson back in Washington on the subject of oil moving from ports to the front, and the problem of an oil supply-shift to the Pacific front, the Secretary asked quaintly if the colonel had found time to visit the 36th Division. The colonel admitted he had and asked the Secretary if he had been informed that the 36th was one of the greatest divisions in the war, having been one of the top three divisions in combat losses.

"I helped train those boys, Mr. Secretary," Ernest said seriously. "A lot of my friends won't come home. My greatest regret is that I was not able to be with them all the way."

CHAPTER XIV

Gas Grows Up

Natural gas and Ernest Thompson have lived a long and eventful life together. Coming out of the Panhandle, as he did, the colonel had an uncommon knowledge of gas even before he reached the Commission. In fact, it was largely responsible for his career. It was the gas issue that aroused his interest in becoming the Mayor of Amarillo. His accomplishment in that position led to his nation-wide publicity and the subsequent call to the Railroad Commission at the time of the East Texas boom.

The colonel's home country of Potter County in the Panhandle was the scene of the first truly great gas dis-covery in 1918. The discovery was at first regarded as a great misfortune. There was no market for gas and it looked as if there were no oil. When the first well came in the operators let it run wide open for days hoping that it would eventually blow in as an oil well. It didn't. By 1934 the Panhandle field had taken over a prominent place in the petroleum spotlight and was estimated to have reserves of twenty trillion cubic feet of gas, and by that time some four trillion feet of gas had already been produced. The field was 115 miles long and twenty miles wide, covering a million-and-a-half acres stretched over seven counties. It became important almost at the same time as did East Texas and, strangely, covered almost an identical amount and shape of acreage. By 1934 there were 727 gas wells and 2000 oil wells which produced much more gas than they did oil. The daily potential of the field was almost twenty billion cubic feet of gas. There were fifteen pipelines taking Panhandle gas to Denver, Chicago, Indianapolis and elsewhere in the Midwest at the rate of more than 300 million cubic feet a day.

The field had fifty-five gasoline plants and twenty-five carbon-black plants. These plants were popping more than 500 million cubic feet of residue gas into the air every day. That was a half-a-billion cubic feet of rank waste of residue gas, a valuable product from nature's storehouse that could never be replaced.

The stubborness of landowners and operators alike was responsible for this wasteful condition. The gas interests had spent millions of dollars to develop markets, lay pipelines and facilities, lease acreage and drill wells between 1926 and 1931. But they were unable to lease the entire reservoir area on their own terms. Approximately twenty percent of the proven gas area lay outside the big companies' leases. The owners of that land held out for better bonuses and royalties, which the companies refused to give.

The only effective gas law on the Texas books when the field came in simply required that a gas well be shut in within ten days after completion until such time as the gas from it could be used for light, fuel or power. That law was passed in 1899.

The minority landowners in the Panhandle field were given legislative relief in 1931 that should have settled the question. The 42nd Texas legislature amended the 1930 Common Purchaser Act for oil to include gas. Under the new law the pipeline companies were required to take gas ratably, or equally, from all wells in the field. The pipeline companies immediately got an injunction against the enforcement of the law as it applied to gas. Thereupon, the legislature passed an amendment to the 1899 gas act which authorized the Railroad Commission to permit the use of gas for any purpose found by the Commission to be practical and conducive to the public welfare.

It might have been the major wars raging on two fronts in the petroleum industry, one in the Panhandle and the other in East Texas, that inspired Governor Sterling to call the colonel in with a view toward his taking over the battle between the gas people. All of the foregoing happened while the colonel was beautifying Amarillo in his peaceful second term as mayor. He had done his best, too, to induce industry to come to Amarillo by offering free gas. Several producers would have gladly furnished anyone with gas, at a price the city government could afford, to get a heating market in order legally to extract the liquid hydrocarbons from the gas. But not one industry ever accepted the offer. Anyway, the call to Austin came and the colonel responded. He hadn't been on the job long before a petition signed by some 6000 Panhandle landowners, royalty owners, laborers, businessmen and other citizens was brought to Austin seeking relief from an intolerable

195

situation. As a result the legislature passed the famous Sour Gas act which authorized producers to use up to twenty-five percent of the potential flow of any gas well for purpose of making gasoline, with the further proviso that the residue could be flared into the air if there were no other market available.

The petitioners contended that gasoline and carbon-black plants in the field had a taxable value of $20 million, produced $14 million annually in products, and hired 2100 men who collected a payroll of almost $4 million a year. And the depression was in full swing. On the other hand the big gas companies provided only $400,000 in royalties and about $200,000 in rentals on undeveloped land each year. The Panhandle citizens believed that these plants provided a practical use of gas and that their contribution to the prosperity of the high plateau country was conducive to the public welfare.

In the meantime the big lines were still in court on a half-dozen or more suits challenging the authority of the legislature, the governor, the attorney general and the Railroad Commission. They had their side of the argument too, and a parade of three-judge federal courts was constantly agreeing with them. The judges understood very little of what they heard but they dashed off rulings and decisions like super-scientists and top technologists.

The Commission issued permits to produce gas for the plants but the big companies slapped another suit on the orders. By 1934 the colonel had been able to get back to Austin occasionally from his pyramidal tent on Proration Hill in East Texas to inject his own legal pyrotechnics where and when needed. Always the commission held out the olive branch with a promise that if and when the pipelines decided to take gas ratably as the law required, that it would then and there stop the gas going to the gasoline and carbon-black plants. The fact of the matter is that that is all the Commission could have done under the law, anyway. Gas could be used for stripping and wasting only if no heat or light market were available. But the big gas companies retained their stubborn attitude and the scandalous waste kept going on. Actually, the plants were utilizing only one-twenty-fourth of the value of the gas. No one ever seemed to object, however, to the fact that the pipelines were selling gas without stripping it of its valuable liquid contents.

The arguments about these gas cases, as well as the East Texas oil injunctions and suits, finally brought the United States Supreme Court to the point of distraction. Justices Black and Douglas, along with others, wrote opinions that, in effect, ordered the lower federal courts to stay out of Texas' oil and gas business. The opinions said that the lower courts were dealing in a realm they were unable to comprehend and, furthermore, that they were subjecting all Texas oil and gas laws to double review. The Supreme Court suggested that the lower federal courts leave the matter to the Texas Railroad Commission and its "working partners," the Texas Courts. After that the nightmare of federal court interference vanished and progress in legislation and regulation was possible.

The colonel spent many weary days before the three-judge federal tribunals before the Supreme Court came to his rescue. He would spend many more in his own state courts but there, at least, the language and the thinking of the Commission, itself a quasi-judicial body, could be understood. In those trying 30's, however, the colonel became fairly well versed in the problems of the natural gas industry.

He decided early that if gas were ever to be developed properly in Texas, there would have to be a good market for the product. Thousands of wells were drilled for oil wherein the operators found only gas. Most gas wells were worse than dry holes. A dry hole could be abandoned. A gas well had to be plugged and watched until a market could be found, which was not very often. Oil operators would find gas but in most cases they would never find a market. It was possible to purchase gas in those days in Texas for almost any price from a cent to three cents a thousand cubic feet. The Commission attempted to encourage gas use by permitting operators to produce virtually unlimited amounts of natural gasoline, distillate or other liquid products from gas so long as the operator had a legitimate market for the residue. Allowables were not applicable in such cases. Some operators were fortunate in finding industries that would take their gas, or tying into one of the gas-utility lines. In most cases, however, gas was a drug on the market. The colonel talked personally with oilmen, both majors and independents, and he made speeches to civic groups, professional men, industrialists and even women's groups and veterans, attempting to impress upon them the importance of natural gas. He encouraged industries to come to Texas and he tried to interest long-line distributors to lay lines from Texas to the East, Midwest or North. John L. Lewis' fight for his union that kept pushing the price of coal up higher and higher delighted the colonel because he felt that if coal got too expensive, gas from Texas would replace it as a fuel. He coined a sales talk in his own inimitable fashion that caught on in newspapers and magazines. He said "Even John L. Lewis cannot tie a housewife to a coal scuttle and an ash can when natural gas and a thermostat will heat her home and cook her meals more efficiently."

It was the colonel's philosophy that the Railroad Commission could not force the saving of gas unless it had value. To make a man spend money saving something that had no value amounted to confiscation, he said. His first job was to attempt to convince his friends in the oil business that gas had a real value. Many men agreed with the colonel but few did anything about it. No man ever did more to try to remove the prejudice, ignorance and timidity about gas. He met head-on the arguments that gas was dangerous, poisonous and deleterious to health generally. His own city was his best showplace because it was one hundred percent gas-fueled with a twenty-five-cent burner tip rate. That was two cents lower than the gas company settled for with him in 1930. The company came back after he was on the Commission and voluntarily asked for a twenty-five-cent rate, the very rate he had first sought. But outside of blowing the front off of Sewall's jewelry store in the heart of town, an episode that caused the colonel some embarrassment and Mr. Sewall some expense, there had never been any trouble with gas in Amarillo. It was a good sales point and he used it frequently, even admitting the jewelry store explosion incident.

"No one was really hurt except the butcher across the street who was picking diamonds and mainsprings out of sausage and round steaks for the next few days," Ernest said.

The colonel preached the need of taking valuable liquids out of gas, putting the gas back into the ground as a pressure maintenance project, and attracting industry to use gas. In Harris County one of the most notable incidents in Texas natural-gas history occured in 1942. As if the war itself were not enough excitement, the Bammel field incident had to come along at the same time.

H. M. Harrell, a Houston oilman, had discovered the field in 1939 and had been producing the gas, stripping it of its liquids, and returning the residue to the reservoir to push out more gas, just as the colonel had been suggesting. He had the entire field, with the exception of one relatively small tract upon which he lost the lease when he did not comply with a drilling obligation. The war needs for industrial Houston opened a gas market rather suddenly; and F. M. Corzelius, another operator, got a gas contract and the lease in Bammel that Mr. Harrell had let lapse. He laid a line to the field and started feeding his pipeline through a second-phase condensate plant that took out some, but by no means all, of the valuable wet gas by-products. Harrell objected to Corzelius' taking volumes of wet gas out of the field and appealed to the Railroad Commission. Since Corzelius was not taking in excess of twenty-five percent of the potential of his well and since he had a fuel market, the Commission could not have stopped him if its membership had been so inclined. Harrell enjoined the Commission from permitting the Corzelius well to operate, but the Texas Supreme Court upheld the Commission's right to adjust the correlative rights in the absence of waste.

Things might have rested there had not the Corzelius well in 1943 developed a serious leak in a faulty casing. The Commission ordered Corzelius to take immediate steps to stop the leak. He complied by pumping water and mud into the well. The well blew out, blew surface soil hundreds of feet into the air, cratered and caught fire. The fire continued unabated through early 1944 by which time the crater covered several acres.

Again the Commission demanded that steps be taken to put out the fire. Corzelius tried. He drilled six relief wells only to wind up with six more blowouts, one of which was of such magnitude that the entire drilling rig, derrick and all equipment disappeared into the crater. To add to Mr. Corzelius' troubles, five of Mr. Harrell's wells caught fire and cratered, too, as the leaking gas escaped into shallow sands and charged them with gas. Mr. Corzelius' troubles did not stop there, however. For several miles around the area, where he had apparently punctured hell, the water wells on farms became geysers spouting water hundreds of feet into the air. Then they turned to gas spouts and some of them ignited. Several farmhouses and some crops burned; and livestock, hunting dogs, pets and chickens were killed. Fissures developed in the land around the area with gas flames pouring out of the ground in long, serpentine streamers.

Corzelius' efforts being worse than merely unsuccessful, the Commission appointed Harrell as its agent to drill a directional hole into the wild well and attempt to shut it off. For some reason Corzelius objected to his competitor killing his well and sued the Commission. The courts held, however, that it was the Commission's duty to prevent waste in any manner possible. The Harrell project succeeded in bringing the blowout under control by pumping cement into the hole for ten hours. In addition to the losses to landowners and operators, the loss of gas amounted to about eight billion cubic feet. The commission, however, gained a new plane of authority by the two important court decisions in its favor.

The colonel's pleas for gas markets began to bear fruit in 1944 when a pipeline to carry Texas gas to the Appalachian region was proposed. But immediately 100 South Texas gas-using industries, fearing the dissipation of their fuel supply, violently opposed the project. They urged the Railroad Commission to stop further exportation of gas out of Texas and promised to study ways to find a profitable use for Texas gas in Texas.

Thompson was convinced that there was already ample gas in the state for a hundred times the number of industries it could possibly attract within the next ten years. In fact his statistics, as early as 1940, had shown there was at least a thirty-year supply for the state. Since then numerous new gas reserves had been tapped. He said there were thousands of oil wells flaring gas all over Texas and that the citizens were disgusted with the waste that was going on.

"It's up to Texas enterprise to attract gas-using industries to Texas," he said, "but I doubt that building a wall around the state will do it. It has only been a very little while since natural gas went begging for outlets, looking for markets in vain. When you say that it should not be permitted to sell Texas gas outside of Texas, then who is going to pay the rentals on the gas lands, and who will pay the development costs? The little operator would be frozen out because he cannot wait for posterity to take his gas.

"We rejoice when a Texas oil field gets a pipeline outlet and we hunt for Texas oil markets all over the globe. Who is going to pay the gas producer to hold his gas for some future local manufacturing demand?" he asked. "The chamber of commerce? The city? The state? The federal government? None of these even contemplate it. If a city wants a gas reserve it can go out and buy it on the competitive market."

Ernest Thompson was convinced that a good market would provide the incentive for further development of gas. He said that no one had ever drilled a well to find gas. All gas discoveries had been accidental, but that with a well-developed market, there would be a gas exploration program equally as vigorous as that for oil. He said that oilmen had begun to realize that gas would some day be as valuable as oil, if not a great deal more so.

But the colonel's pleas did not convince even his colleagues. Olin Culberson said that large volumes of gas should not be exported to other states. He advocated keeping it in Texas and letting the industries come where this great fuel and raw material was plentiful. He urged promotion of factories and plants from one end of the State to another by refusing to let other states profit from Texas' great resource. Culberson was particularly disturbed over long-term contracts that would tie up Texas gas for fifteen or twenty years. Beauford Jester, the newest commissioner, was a potential candidate for governor. Whether that fact had any bearing on his attitude or not, he was inclined to go along with Culberson and the one hundred South Texas industries. The idea of Culberson and Jester—to hold a bridle on gas destined for export from Texas—was not based on conservation but on a "Texas First" attitude. The colonel could see their point but he firmly believed that unless there was a policy of freedom of gas there would always be a hesitancy on the part of large transmission lines to invest millions in markets and facilities. Culberson warned against fifteen- and twenty-year contracts, but Thompson was convinced that unless transmission lines were able to obtain such dedicated reserves they could not possibly assure prospective markets of a continuing supply. The Culberson-Jester arguments were far more popular with Texans, especially important segments of the press and local chambers of commerce. The colonel was unwilling to retreat. Instead, he pushed his point in the face of all pressure and even political threats.

In the spring of 1946 Beauford Jester became a candidate for governor. His principal opponent was Dr. Homer Rainey, former president of the University of Texas. That was the race in which Jerry Sadler, the commissioner who resigned to go into the army, made his political exit. The run-off saw Jester and Rainey pitted against each other in a bitter battle, but Jester came out with a sound victory.

Shortly after Jester became governor, he appointed William J. Murray to his position on the Railroad Commission. Murray was one of the chief technical men on the Commission staff. He was a trained petroleum engineer and the first man with such qualifications ever to serve on the regulatory body. Murray had been given his first job on the Commission by Smith and Sadler, two men who seldom agreed with the colonel. And, of course, he was appointed to the Commission by Jester who, although he was on Thompson's side on almost everything else, opposed the colonel's policy of freedom of gas. The new, young, intelligent and vigorous commissioner became a Thompson free gas advocate almost immediately.

Within a short time the use which the colonel had suggested for the Big Inch and Little Inch pipelines even before they were built had become a reality. They were purchased by the Texas Eastern Pipeline Company and converted into gas lines to transport Texas gas to the Eastern seaboard. In the meantime other important gas transmission companies started a program of construction and expansion. The impetus of new markets with good prices for gas did exactly what the colonel had anticipated. Independents and majors alike started exploring for gas instead of running into it accidentally while drilling for oil.

The colonel's persistence and vision had again opened an entirely new field of opportunity for the petroleum industry. Land and lease values increased, state revenue prospects improved, an expected postwar lull in drilling and exploration failed to materialize, and Texas gas reserves began to increase by leaps and bounds. And, above all, the housewives in the East, Midwest, and even the Far West, started to cut the ties that bound them to the coal scuttle and the ashpan.

CHAPTER XV

New Horizons in Conservation

It was logical to assume, and most industry leaders did assume, that with the end of the war there would be a period of serious overproduction of oil. Fighting planes were grounded, ships were coming home to rest at anchor, tanks and trucks and other military vehicles were being parked in deserts and in vast government yards, and fire bombs and flame throwers had rendered their final lethal service.

But Ernest Thompson, whose vision was long and whose voice was loud and clear, believed otherwise. In the first place, the war had taken a serious toll of natural resources. In the immediate postwar period, he said, people would fill up their starved gasoline tanks and take the long vacations they had been forced to by-pass for five years. Furthermore, civilian air travel would have phenomenal growth, millions of new cars would be rushed off the assembly lines, mechanized divisions would be replaced by mechanized farms and there would be a great demand for oil for home heating, and for industrial plants. He also foresaw a tremendous upsurge in the petroleum chemical industry which would require vast amounts of oil and gas. Ernest Thompson was no pessimist.

His predictions came true with such amazing accuracy that oil was soon in short supply instead of being overproduced. The Office of Price Administration kept its thumb pressed down hard on crude-oil prices. There was little incentive to wildcat for oil or to develop existing fields. The colonel constantly pleaded with Washington to be realistic and permit a fair price for oil and to do something to provide the necessary steel for the industry. The Office of Price Administration grudgingly permitted an ineffectual ten-cent price increase for crude in April of 1946. In July, oil was decontrolled and a twenty-five-cent price increase resulted. This incentive spurred drilling activity as much as the steel shortage would permit. But heavy demand, strikes and gray-market chiselers still made steel scarce.

Scientific and technological development in the petroleum industry had taken tremendous steps forward during the war years in spite of the obstacles. But with the coming of peace far greater things were to come. Behind each of them was the helping hand of Ernest Thompson, his colleagues on the powerful Texas Railroad Commission, and the regulatory leaders in the Interstate Oil Compact states.

Many engineering studies of oil and gas reservoirs had been made to determine the maximum efficient rate (MER) of production for each field and the producing horizon in each field. The colonel had long advocated what the industry came to know as MER. The major companies had started investing great fortunes in research for engineering, geology and geophysics. Molecular magicians began to take hydrocarbons and juggle their molecules to create thousands of new uses for petroleum, particularly the lighter hydrocarbons which previously had been useful only as fuel.

Conservation had advanced to the point where both oil and gas fields were being opened with amazing efficiency. However, the colonel knew one area where all had not been done that could be done. He believed that casing-head gas had to be conserved and he knew that it would take drastic action to accomplish that purpose. He talked about gas flares to individuals and groups on any occasion. Soon the word was picked up by the press. Laymen started complaining about the terrible waste. They wanted to know why the state would permit millions, even billions of cubic feet of gas to escape daily out of Texas oil wells. Why, they asked, wasn't that gas used. The colonel had planted those questions and soon a chorus of voices was echoing them from one side of the State to the other.

There had to be a start. In 1946 the Railroad Commission held a hearing on the Seeligson field in Nueces county on the Texas coast and asked the operators to show cause why gas flaring should not be stopped in the field. The operators asked for more time and the meeting was recessed for one year. The companies had plans for co-operatively building a gasoline-extraction plant. A year later the meeting was reconvened and it was found that the gas was still being vented into the air. The amount was about thirty-eight million cubic feet of gas a day. The colonel explained that the gas was not totally lost since it had served the important purpose of lifting the oil produced in the field. But he deplored the subsequent unnecessary waste. As soon as the meeting closed the Railroad Commission wrote one of the most revolutionary orders in Texas oil history. It ordered Seeligson field shut in except for wells that were using casinghead gas for light, fuel or carbon black, or returning it to the producing horizon. The companies got an injunction on the grounds that the order was unreasonable. The Commission appealed to the State Supreme Court, which upheld the Commission order. The Supreme Court sent the case back, however, to the lower court to determine whether or not the volume of waste was sufficient to justify the shutdown. The lower court sustained the Commission and the order was allowed to stand. The operators begged further delay to complete their plant. The request was allowed and soon the plant was in operation recovering 1200 barrels of liquids daily and delivering the residue gas to a transmission line.

This case was used as an example of what could be done and the colonel never missed an opportunity to bring its good results to public attention.

With petroleum short it was not logical to shut in other fields immediately, but other operators were fairly well warned of what was going to happen and many started taking action. In the meantime the colonel waged a campaign against the use of high-octane gasoline by automobile drivers, contending that it was an unnecessary waste of a valuable resource because it took more crude to make it and did not get more mileage or power from properly adjusted cars.

In 1947 he warned the American Petroleum Institute that crude demand would continue to rise and he predicted a national demand of six million barrels a day. That, he said, would be 400,000 barrels above MER (maximum efficient rate of recovery) and that more discoveries were needed. An urgent meeting of the Commission was held in July of 1947 at the request of several crude purchasers to urge an increase in Texas allowables. Gasoline demand was up thirteen percent over 1946, and several labor strikes in the oil and steel industries had been most harmful. Texas allowables were raised 90,000 barrels a day. The colonel appeared before a Congressional committee and said that any gasoline shortage could be cured by making steel available for drilling, raising crude prices to stimulate wildcatting, encouraging public use of lower octane gasoline, and by the encouragement of secondary recovery methods in old, wastefully produced oil fields. He answered hundreds of miscellaneous questions and insisted that the industry was not running out of oil since reserves were at an all-time high. He urged steel for refineries and more pipelines.

Old Ocean was a fabulous oil field southwest of Houston in Brazoria County. The colonel had taken a particular interest in it because his friend Jim Abercrombie had been one of the discoverers. Back in 1938, F. W. Fisher, the "Big Fish" of East Texas, had come to complain of the large allowables the few wells in the field had been granted. Jerry Sadler had invited him.

Fisher had compared East Texas' twenty barrels with the 200 barrels a day allowed in Old Ocean. He had called it a rank injustice. Abercrombie had been called by the colonel to reply. Abercrombie told the Commission about the problems of drilling 10,000 feet and deeper into terrific pressures, and the failures that had occurred before he himself had invented a giant valve that would control the pressures. He showed that one Old Ocean well cost as much as twenty wells in East Texas where every well was assured. In Old Ocean every well was a gamble; it might produce and it might not. It was a job of pioneering in Gulf Coast depths never before attempted. Abercrombie said that he, too, was an East Texas producer but that he was able to make more money out of a twenty-barrel well in the middle of the Black Giant than he could make out of a 200-barrel well in Old Ocean. Without a minimum allowable of 200 barrels it would not be possible, he said, to drill in Old Ocean. Yet below the land around the San Bernard River there lay a great reserve that could serve mankind. When he had finished Sadler turned to his witness and asked if he had any further questions. "If you haven't, Mr. Fisher," Sadler said, "it looks as if you have lost a case." The "Big Fish" smiled and said nothing. He knew it would be ridiculous to ask for equal allowables in the two fields. Jim Abercrombie had justified the colonel's confidence in his pioneering. The criticism and the pressure were off the colonel in another landmark case of conservation.

Under Abercrombie, Dan Harrison, E. DeGolyer, W. H. Hodnett and several others, Old Ocean became a great oil field. It was later unitized by the new operators and became a model oil field. A gasoline-extraction plant was built there because great volumes of gas came up in solution with the golden-colored crude. In 1945 it was suggested that the landowners also unitize their interests, and the Old Ocean Royalty Owners Association was organized. The landowners engaged Michel T. Halbouty, a capable and vigorous young petroleum engineer and geologist who had recently returned from active duty as chief of the production division of the Joint Chiefs of Staff's war advisory board. Halbouty worked out the first large unit operations for landowners in the state and one that would later serve as a model.

In September of 1947 Old Ocean became the second field to be ordered to stop flaring gas. The order was issued early in September to become effective October 1. On the effective date the operators announced that the order had been followed one hundred percent. The gas that had been put through the extraction plant was not being flared any longer. It was being reinjected into the producing horizons to assist in maintaining the pressure to assure the production of more oil and gas. It was the first successful operation of its kind in the state, not only from the standpoint of being a double-unit operation, but from the standpoint of not having any of its products wasted. It was one of the greatest models of conservation in the nation. And behind every step of its progress toward that point had been Colonel Thompson.

In 1947 there were spot fuel-oil and gasoline shortages about the nation but the colonel laid the blame on transportation facilities. He said in August that Texas was exceeding the Bureau of Mines estimates for the state and producing 2,283,500 barrels daily. He said there was no oil problem that pipe and price could not cure. By the end of the year all Texas wells were producing at maximum under MER, which had become an adopted standard. By the end of the year the Commission was able to report that two-and-a-half billion barrels of new reserves had been discovered in an all-time record of 160 new fields for the state. The colonel reported that all Texas wells "are not producing as much as they could but are producing as much as they should. That's MER in a nutshell." To dramatize his point he said that many wells in the state were capable of producing 30,000 barrels a day but that the average daily allowable was twenty-six barrels per well.

The colonel took time out from his busy schedule to announce his support of President Truman for re-election at a Jefferson Day dinner in Santa Fe, New Mexico. He said the President's program had been largely responsible for maintaining high levels of employment. Early in 1948 he praised the Marshall Plan as a way to keep Europe from becoming Communist. He said aid to Turkey and Greece was important since those nations stood between Russian and twenty-six billion barrels of oil in the Middle East. He described the Middle East oil as a providential asset in securing the freedom of the world by supplying Europe and taking that load off America. But he was critical of the United States' policy of taking great quantities of steel for Middle East refineries and pipelines, thereby depriving domestic producers.

The summer of 1948 brought the colonel's name to the polls again. He won in the first primary with the largest majority in his political career. He hardly missed a beat from his busy schedule to make a political speech. The people of Texas had recognized the fact that his presence on the regulatory body that controlled their most vital industry was essential to the welfare of the state. His majority was tremendous in every one of the 254 counties of the state.

The early winter months of 1948 saw a serious lack of fuel oil for the East Coast in one of the hardest winters in history. A Congressman from Massachusettes gave the oil industry a week to solve the problem on the threat of introducing a federal-control bill. Thompson replied that the shortage was in pipeline transportation due to the huge steel shipments to the Middle East. He said Texas was producing at an all-time high of 2,433,000 barrels a day. A suggestion of rationing was met by his argument that regular gas instead of premium gas be used by automobile drivers.

At Bradford, Pennsylvania, where he was inspecting new methods in secondary recovery of oil, the colonel made a speech and amazed his listeners by telling of Texas wells going down as deep as 17,000 feet with 20,000-foot wells in the near future. He said such wells cost from a half-million to a million dollars to drill and more than half of them were coming in dry. He said the state was taking a new interest in research. Of course,

215

he had been one of the fathers of petroleum research, encouraging and pushing every feasible idea that he came across.

That month, also, the Texas Commission re-examined the MER of every well in Texas to see if production could be increased. This program paid good dividends. Senator Lyndon Johnson congratulated Thompson on the Commission's MER program in April, and said he would support government aid for secondary recovery and research in drilling technique. Johnson said that in the event of war the nation would need eight million barrels of oil a day as contrasted with existing production levels of five-and-a-half million barrels. Johnson said the seriousness of the petroleum supply situation could not be over-emphasized and that Congress was calling on the steel industry to give primary consideration to oil needs. He also mentioned the necessity of imports on a supplementary basis, and the hope that Congress would quit-claim the tidelands to the states.

Everything in the letter echoed pleas the colonel had been making. He took the liberty of giving it to the press.

Secretary of the Interior Krug, who had succeeded Harold Ickes, had announced officially that gasoline rationing would not be needed and that the oil industry need have no fears of any other federal controls. Early in September the colonel addressed the Interstate Oil Compact Commission's quarterly meeting in New York. The number of member states had grown to twenty-two by that time. He took the occasion to recall the prophets of doom who had previously shouted for federal control and had predicted, in 1932, that the nation would be out of oil in fourteen years, or by 1946. He said that in that time the industry had doubled its production and increased its reserves by seventy-five percent with state jealousies giving way to interstate co-operation. He was a proud parent, with his friends Elwood Fouts and James V. Allred, of the simple document that was the foundation of the Compact.

A few days later, addressing the national convention of the Independent Petroleum Association of America, he urged the prompt development of the tidelands, stressing the great need for the reserves that would not be touched as long as the federal government continued to cloud the titles.

"Experience has shown that the best oil development is under state control. We cannot risk the chance of letting the palsied hand of federal control dry up oil development on our tidelands," he told the independents.

By the last quarter of 1948 the oil supply shortage was over, but the Railroad Commission kept allowables high. In the meantime oil stocks were building up. The Seeligson field was operating through its new plant and putting residue gas back into the producing horizons. The example of Old Ocean had had its effect. And the talk of stopping flare gas in other fields continued. The colonel seldom missed a chance to point to the wasteful torches that lit the countryside. On November 23 the Commission hit the front pages all over Texas with an order shutting down sixteen more fields including such important producing areas as Conroe, Heyser, Flour Bluff and Wasson. No one in the industry had a good reason to be surprised since the Seeligson and Old Ocean warnings, but twenty-five companies sought injunctions immediately. Attorney General Price Daniel pointed out to the courts that nearly 120 billion cubic feet of gas a year would continue to be lost unless the injunctions were voided. Then, on December 13, the Commission announced a hearing for late January at which operators in twenty-five more fields, including the great East Texas field, would be called on to show cause why they should not be closed down until flaring could be eliminated. The colonel said 177 million cubic feet of gas daily was the issue involved.

Letters of congratulations came from the North Texas Oil and Gas Association and others. The Independent Petroleum Association of Texas, through its president, D. Harold Byrd, strongly supported the elimination of flaring. Thompson was proud of the part of Byrd's letter to him which stated:

"Those of us in the oil and gas producing business should consider ourselves as occupying a position of trust; that we are partners with the people of Texas in developing and marketing our natural resources in an orderly, economical manner . . . not in exploiting Texas."

There was little trouble in the courts over the shutdowns. Precedents had been set. The people had been conditioned. The oil was not needed because the shortage had been met magnificently by the industry.

In fact the oil shortage was so definitely over that the Texas Railroad Commission cut state allowables 250,000 barrels a day on January 1. In February an additional 66,000 barrels were cut. Imports were flooding into the country and, for the first time in twenty-five years, America had become a net importer of oil. By April Texas allowables had been cut 750,000 barrels a day and many independent oilmen were beginning to fall by the wayside under the pressure. The ironic fact was that these necessary reductions in the face of excessive imports were made at a time when national demand was at an all-time high.

Early in January the colonel had warned of the potential danger of excessive imports.

"Imports should supplement but not supplant domestic oil," he said at Spindletop at the anniversary services at the famous Lucas Monument.

The colonel said that supply had caught up with and passed demand and that butane and other liquid petroleum gases were supplying over five million homes in the nation with a product that was formerly flared into the air. He said the Middle East oil was a great blessing but also a grave danger. The colonel amazed his audience by revealing that the Middle East had reserves estimated at thirty-four billion barrels compared with the United States' twenty-four billion barrels. He said that whereas Texas wells were averaging twenty-three barrels a day under proration, the Middle East wells were averaging about 8000 barrels a day without being harmed since all of the casing-head gas was being reinjected. He said the foreign fields were producing a half-million barrels of oil daily with only sixty-six wells and in only three oil fields. The colonel did not denounce the imports. But he pleaded that the thing not be overdone and that the great fields, mostly operated by Americans, continue to be a blessing, instead of a destructive force against the domestic oil industry in the United States.

By the time the Commission had been forced to cut allowables by three-quarters of a million barrels daily in Texas, the colonel told the House Small Business Committee meeting in Dallas that imports were the most serious threat to small oilmen. He said he believed it was time for the importing companies to realize that they were going too far and he appealed to them to use "business statesmanship" before it was too late. A committee report accused the oil industry of two faults. First, it accused the industry of not supplying enough oil in 1946 and 1947. Second, it accused the Commission of not eliminating flaring earlier. Thompson replied that Texas had produced all the oil the Bureau of Mines estimates had required each month until the import situation had forced a cutback. Then he said that if the Commission had stopped flaring gas sooner, the oil shortage would have been worse since in most fields it was impossible to produce oil without the gas to lift it. The Commission, he pointed out, waited until the shortage was over to close in the flaring fields.

"The committee report seems confused," the colonel commented with great charity.

By 1949 the gas-well operators were beginning to become apprehensive of federal control. Certain powers in Washington had hinted that since the big gas-transmission lines were subject to federal control, the producers supplying them should be subject to the same controls. The authors of the 1938 Federal Gas Act said their intent was to exempt producers who sold gas "at arms length" to the interstate companies. Senator Kerr offered a bill to clarify the original law, and strong opposition arose. The colonel was called to testify on the Kerr bill and he did the usual good job. But the committee, fascinated as all Congressional committees always were by this man's knowledge of the industry, veered from the subject and started asking unrelated questions. Thompson remarked that those who said the country was running out of oil were misinformed. He also said that gas was in plentiful supply but that the price would rise because it was far more valuable than its present price. Wildcatting for gas, the colonel told the committeemen, would increase with the rising prices and add to the reserves. He surprised the committee with the assertion that wildcatters had invested far more money drilling dry holes than they had recovered from production on the whole. He quoted the unbelievable costs of drilling exploratory wells and the tremendous odds against hitting. Costs ranged up to a million dollars a well and the chances of success ranged up to almost one in a thousand for a major discovery. The Kerr bill passed only to be vetoed by President Truman.

Conservation and elimination of waste became a religion with the colonel. In every drop of oil and every cubic foot of gas he could see a value to his fellow man. He could see, too, that once that drop or that cubic foot was used or lost that it could never be recovered. To use it was the purpose for which God had placed it in the great reservoirs, he reasoned. To fail to recover it, or to permit its loss was, in the eyes of the colonel, a cardinal sin. His gift was not one of scientific discovery or tech-

221

nological know-how. But he was able to recognize those gifts in other men and was in a position to encourage them and give them official aid.

Such was the case when engineers proposed putting gas back into the producing horizons for the purpose of maintaining pressure that would assure the maximum efficient rate of recovery for hydrocarbons. That is why he left no stone unturned to eliminate wasteful flaring. His contribution was to all concerned because it meant more reward for the land and royalty owners, producers and refiners, and more available energy for America's progress and prosperity.

When a group of pioneers had foreseen the great disaster that would come from 30,000 East Texas wells all producing many times as much salt water as they did oil, they immediately had the support of Ernest Thompson. Through every step of their program, which started even before there was salt water in the field, the colonel was at their side. He and his colleagues issued orders to give them aid, offered oil allowable bonuses to help finance their efforts, and saw to it that all men in the industry could profit by their experience. Without those men, who represented fifteen far-sighted producing companies in the field, East Texas might have stalled at the halfway point and the people might have lost the use of some three billion or more barrels of oil.

Colonel Thompson had been fascinated on his visit to Bradford, Pennsylvania by the manner in which operators there were flooding oil reservoirs with water to force previously lost oil out the top of the well bores. He saw water-injection wells drilled in a pattern that put water wells on four sides of each oil well. That water would crowd in on the oil from all sides and force it, under hydrostatic pressure, into the bottom of the well bore from which point it would find its way up the tubing, out the well head and into the tanks. The extremely high value of Pennsylvania crude made that operation profitable even where the results were no greater than a half a barrel a day.

When he returned to Texas he talked with his colleagues about the idea and they agreed with him that encouragement should be given anyone who would try such a plan anywhere in Texas. The first applicant for such aid was a group of Pennsylvania men in the Forrest Oil Company who were willing to try the experiment in the almost depleted South Ward field in Ward County. The colonel asked where, in the parched lands of West Texas, the operators proposed to get sufficient water to carry on a water flooding program. The men had the answer ready. They would tap the Rustler sand at 700 feet and reinject it into the oil-producing Penn Bennett sand at 2400 feet. They asked the Commission what allowables they could expect if they undertook an expensive water-flooding project. Thompson, Culberson and Murray all agreed that they would first write an order permitting the program; and second, they would allow all of the oil that could be recovered from each well every day without limit. That was the incentive the operators needed. They tried the plan and it worked perfectly. Instead of two or three barrels daily from wells in the South Ward reservoir, they were getting several hundred barrels a day from each well. Their initiative and investment paid off and thousands of barrels of oil that might have otherwise been lost were produced. In sixteen months the field produced more oil by water flooding than was recovered in the primary flowing and pumping stages in twenty-one years.

The East Texas plan to dispose of salt water brought another type of pressure-maintenance operation which was not fully expected. The salt water injected into the Woodbine sand on the west side of the field provided a new hydrostatic head to the sand. It followed a relatively straight line across the field with the water table replacing the oil as it moved east but maintaining the pressures at an almost even figure. This eliminated the necessity for standard pumping equipment and kept the wells flowing. It is estimated that, due to the practical oilmen who conceived the idea, the chemists who saved it from failure, and the encouragement of the colonel and his colleagues, the field would produce almost ninety percent of all of the oil in the sand.

There are no laws in Texas which directly authorize an owner or operator of any well to inject air, gas or water for the purpose of recovering more hydrocarbons from a reservoir. The Railroad Commission authorizes such operations under its regulatory powers.

It encourages water flooding as it did in East Texas and South Ward by bonuses in allowables, orders when and where needed, and counsel and advice. It penalizes those who would waste gas by flaring it, instead of rejecting it back into the reservoir in the absence of a market, by shutting in fields until flaring is discontinued where that is possible. The Commission has always applied the rule of reason, the colonel's favorite philosophy, in cases of undue hardship. Gas that comes up with oil is not entirely waste, the colonel argues. It has lifted oil. Therefore when an isolated well or a small group of wells is unable to either find a market for gas or afford an expensive program of repressuring, there is no order of penalty.

The immediate postwar years brought great problems to the Texas oil industry. The colonel reasoned that the successful solutions, or the wrong answers, would affect the entire national output since the dominant position of Texas oil and gas to the nation requires its leadership in conservation and waste prevention. Aware of that responsibility of leadership the colonel and his fellow commissioners, although frequently differing in minor matters, always worked together to provide the answers to the major problems.

CHAPTER XVI

No Greater Influence

The colonel picked up the afternoon newspaper on August 21, 1948 and learned that he was a major general. Governor Beauford Jester, his former Commission colleague and World War I comrade in the 90th Division, had made the appointment. Jester had planned a surprise ceremony for the colonel, but a reporter learned about the promotion and wrote the story prematurely. With his new rank he became deputy commander of the Texas National Guard.

Nine months later there were three stars for the colonel. Only two months before Beauford Jester became the first governor of Texas to die in office, he appointed Thompson commander of the Texas National Guard and promoted him to lieutenant general. For Ernest it was an honor equal to that of becoming governor. It compensated too, for the disappointment of having missed wartime service with his regiment.

In spite of the fact that he was a fine figure of a man in his new uniform and the three stars, his old friends still addressed him as "colonel." They reserved the higher rank for formal occasions, public speeches or appearances before Congress. Those close to Ernest would always call him colonel and he preferred it. He had won that rank and title on the field of combat and he cherished it above any other possession.

As usual, Amarillo was proud of its favorite son. More than 1500 friends from twenty-two states attended a barbecue to pay tribute to Ernest. Later the Amarillo Rotary Club, of which he was a local founder, made him a distinguished life member. When Oil Progress Week came around the *Globe-News* issued a complete special edition dedicated to the town's hero. To Amarillo, he *was* oil progress. This son of old Rag Town was no prophet without honor in his own home town. Amarillo remembered him when he was a mascot and then a trooper for the local National Guard. Now the redhead was chief of the entire Guard and he seemed to wear his three stars well.

But there were other things to consider in 1949 besides honors. That was the year foreign imports first became a major postwar problem. It was also the year the finishing touch was put to an Anglo-American Oil Treaty that had been proposed during the war year of 1944 by the State Department. At first the proponents had obtained the colonel's endorsement to the Treaty. They had represented it as merely an extension, on an international basis, of the Interstate Oil Compact Commission plan. Then Thompson discovered the Treaty would create an international organization to set oil quotas, fix prices, regulate production, dictate engineering practices, and virtually legalize international oil cartels. He did an about-face and openly attacked the Treaty. A veiled offer to make him the directing head of the international regulatory body to be created by the Treaty failed to win his essential support.

In effect, the Treaty was another attempt by certain politicians in Washington and a few industry leaders to bring about federal control in a new and devious manner. Beauford Jester had seen the true implications early and had suggested that independent oilmen, especially, take up arms against the move. One of the independent oil associations created a strong committee headed by Glenn McCarthy of Houston and Grady Vaughan of Dallas. Thompson was a constant source of ammunition in the anti-Treaty movement and frequently took up a position at the head of the fight. The year 1949 marked the end of the controversy, when the Senate Foreign Relations Committee finally let the proposal die in the committee in spite of tremendous pressure from the administration for its ratification.

The year of 1949 also brought the colonel one of his major achievements when the Texas Petroleum Research Committee was established by the heads of Texas University and Texas A. and M. College. The colonel was named chairman of the steering committee with the president of the University and the chancellor of A. and M. as the other members. The purpose of the committee, as long advocated by Thompson, was to encourage student research projects in petroleum engineering with particular emphasis on secondary recovery problems and improvement in primary oil-recovery methods. William J. Murray, Jr., another member of the Texas Railroad Commission, was named to head the research committee which also included two engineering professors from Texas University and two from A. and M. College.

With each passing day the influence of Ernest Thompson was felt more and more in the oil and gas industry. By 1950 he was its spokesman, not only in Texas, but almost everywhere. The freckle-faced boy from Rag Town, the heroic colonel of the 90th Division, the fighting Mayor of Amarillo, and the determined captain of Proration Hill had earned his position. With Murray and Culberson as his colleagues, he was part of one of the most formidable state bodies that ever served a people. The industry and the government both looked to Ernest Thompson for guidance. His voice was one of experience and integrity. His only interest was in a greater take from God's reservoirs for the people of his state and nation. He recognized the genius and the ability of petroleum's leaders with whom he walked and lived. And those men recognized in him a leader and a national, even world-wide, umpire who never deviated from his course. The colonel had long since given up the practice of law, but he was still a hotel man and office-building owner. The fact that he held no oil interest whatsoever was no accident. He had turned down thousands of opportunities to get into the oil business where he undoubtedly would have become a fabulous success. But he looked on his job as a lifework far more important. His office building and his two hotels, the Amarillo and the Herring, were enjoying all of the prosperity he needed.

President Truman called on the colonel again in 1951 to represent him at the World Petroleum Congress. Again he accepted gladly. May accompanied him, as did his old technical adviser, R. W. Byram. Colonel Lawrence Hagy of Amarillo also went along. Dr. William Embry Wrather, chief of the United States Geological Survey, was the other American delegate to the Congress. The colonel's greatest contribution was to reassure the British that the Americans had no intention of moving in on the troubled Iranian oil scene. Upon his return Ernest Thompson made a magnificent report to Secretary of State Acheson on the world oil situation. The most startling part of the report was that slightly more than half of the world oil reserves of ninety-five billion barrels were located in the Middle East. He reminded the Secretary, however, that the 150 million Americans consumed two-thirds of the world's oil. He got in plugs for conservation, the depletion allowance, domestic production and the Interstate Oil Compact Commission.

The trip to Europe was almost disastrous. The colonel became seriously ill while in The Hague, and it was several months before he was able to be completely active again. His illness threw a scare into the oil industry as well as government leaders. Some realized for the first time that the loss of this great public servant could bring far greater chaos to the industry and its chances of making a major contribution to world peace than anything else. For the weeks he was in a Houston hospital hundreds of anxious calls and personal inquiries from every part of the nation and many foreign countries indicated the tremendous respect the oil world had for this quietly effective and scholarly man who had been more instrumental than any other single individual in stabilizing the industry.

Before many weeks had passed, however, the redhead from Amarillo was back on his feet talking before oil meetings, in classrooms, to women's clubs, before Congressional committees and in banquet halls. His simple and graphic style of explaining the complexities of the most complicated of all industries was a source of constant amazement.

The recognition that had long been due the colonel came on the evening of November 7, 1951 in the Grand Ballroom of the Conrad Hilton Hotel in Chicago. W. Alton Jones, president of the American Petroleum Institute, made the presentation. It was the Gold Medal for Distinguished Achievement, petroleum's equivalent of the Nobel Prize which had gone to only five recipients before in the industry's long history. Among those had been Henry Ford for making the automobile the popular vehicle of transportation in America; Charles I. Kettering, whose self-starter had doubled the use of the automobile and made it possible for women to drive it; and Dr. W. M. Burton whose thermal cracking process had enabled the recovery of twice as much gasoline from a barrel of oil as had formerly been obtained.

"The recipient is known to every one of you here," Alton Jones said in introducing the colonel. "His name looms large on every roster of petroleum pioneers and statesmen. His influence upon the orderly development of a great natural resource has been second to that of no man."

The colonel sat quietly through the ceremony and the introduction. His friend Jim Abercrombie sat at his side and patted him on the back as he went forth to receive the award. He accepted the medal and the beautiful parchment scroll with great humility, "in the name of oil and gas conservation and for the good work of conservation officials everywhere."

His speech of acceptance was a typical Thompson masterpiece of human interest. For the first time he revealed that his first interest in the challenging theory of reservoir behavior had come from Henry L. Doherty in 1924.

"He talked to me all night about it right after a committee of oilmen in Fort Worth had refused to hear him on the subject," Thompson told his audience. "I had to listen. He was my client and I didn't have many. I rode from Fort Worth to St. Louis as he talked. My bags were on the car to Amarillo, but I didn't want to stop listening to Mr. Doherty. In fact, I probably couldn't have if I had wanted to. But his great idea of reservoir control fascinated me. It helped to guide me through the wilderness of East Texas."

The colonel took the occasion to predict that domestic oil consumption in the United States would be somewhere between twelve and fourteen million barrels a day by 1975, more than double the demand forecast for 1952.

A few months later the Interstate Oil Compact Commission was holding its quarterly meeting in Phoenix. The colonel was there in his role as chairman of the legal committee. At his invitation Antonio J. Bermudez, suave, handsome, able and dedicated director general of Pemex, Mexico's petroleum administration, was present as an honored guest. That was an achievement toward the colonel's movement for hemispheric solidarity for oil. Mexico was still regarded with misgivings by American oilmen, a condition that resulted from the 1938 expropriation of all foreign oil properties by that government.

Ernest Thompson was convinced that the security of the world might lie in the proper development of the Western Hemisphere and that the most important project in that development was oil and gas. He believed in the sovereignty of each nation as he did in the rights of each state. His hope, however, was that the pitfalls of waste experienced in this country and in the earlier oil history of Mexico could be avoided. Thompson wanted the Western Hemisphere oil-producing nations to be in the Interstate Oil Compact as observers and participants. Canada had already heard his call and had a better conservation law than Texas. Venezuela, whose government had invited him on an official visit, was participating already. Mexico, the colonel reasoned, needed the Compact as much as the Compact needed Mexico.

Señor Bermudez and his official staff were accorded the full hospitality of the delegates at the Westward Ho Hotel. The director general of Pemex was introduced and invited to say a few words.

His response was a brilliant expression of democratic principles, an assurance of Mexico's intention to take its place in the development of natural resources and in the colonel's program of solidarity for the hemisphere.

Then, turning toward the colonel, Señor Bermudez said he felt certain Mexico would go along with anything that had Ernest Thompson's approval.

"General Thompson," he said, "has dedicated his life to his work with complete devotion to duty and with utter lack of selfishness. His leadership in oil and gas conservation has benefited all mankind throughout the world, but particularly in America and in this hemisphere. I know my people will follow his advice. They respect great men."

The words of the Mexican statesman stirred the meeting. The delegates, including seven state governors, gave the Compact's most important founding father a tremendous ovation that lasted until he stood and acknowledged it.

The next month he was in Venezuela. He was the guest of the President and the Ministry of Mines and Hydrocarbons. He visited the new hospital, university, trade schools and air terminals as well as the vast oil fields, and was told that the country had a debt of less than $3 per capita.

"All of this," he said to his old friend Leroy Menzing of the *Fort Worth Star Telegram*, "has come from oil. The proper development of natural resources will bring the same prosperity to all of South and Central America eventually."

One of the men to meet the colonel's plane when it landed in Venezuela was Jack Baumel, chief engineer of the Texas Railroad Commission who has been on loan to the Ministry of Mines and Hydrocarbons there for several years.

As the postwar period settled into second gear the oil industry was facing an old problem in a new wrapper. America had long since ceased to be a net exporter of oil. Its great demand had necessitated imports. As early as 1950 the import problem had become serious. It threatened again to split the industry into two warring factions.

The problem was not a simple one. In order to keep the great oil reserves of the Middle East from falling into enemy hands, the United States had encouraged American investments and development there. No one, of course, had anticipated the incredible results. Oil was found in quantities that dwarfed the Black Giant of East Texas. There had to be an outlet for the oil. America was the market. In periods of strain on production, Middle East oil imports began to mount. By 1950 they were a serious burden. There was no governmental agency to control the situation. None of the importers knew what their competitors were going to do, and all of them wanted to get their investments out of the Middle East as soon as possible. As imports mounted, domestic oil allowables were cut down. Independent oil producers were caught in the squeeze. Loans made on anticipated steady or expanding demands were not being met. Wildcatters, the backbone of the domestic industry, were going broke as their properties were being foreclosed by insurance companies and other financial institutions.

One segment of the industry, composed largely of independent producers, started a movement for a quota on imports to be set by an Act of Congress. Importers believed that some government agency should be established to make forecasts of foreign oil needs by which the companies could be guided.

Ernest Thompson warned against either move. He saw in both the threat of federal control. His pleas were for importers to "supplement but not supplant" domestic production. He urged the executives of the importing companies to use "business statesmanship." With the problem growing by leaps and bounds he went to the public. At times he almost lost his patience with some of the importers. At other times he criticized independents who lined themselves up with the coal interests and John L. Lewis to back an import quota law.

Finally, the colonel and his two colleagues decided on a course that would help solve the problem. The importing companies were requested to file with the Texas Railroad Commission each month an estimate of their anticipated imports. The colonel warned the importers that the state's conservation laws, the most important stabilizing force in the oil industry, would be jeopardized by continuing allowable reductions and to be guided accordingly. The influence of the colonel and his colleagues has had considerable effect and might eventually be the one court of last resort in solving the problem.

Ernest Thompson's voice has been most effective in protecting the twenty-seven and one-half percentage depletion allowance for oil producers. His interest in that subject is the same as his interest in all subjects pertaining to petroleum and its conservation. It serves the public. Without the percentage depletion, the colonel contends there would be no wildcatters. The depletion is the lure of gain that attracts them into taking almost impossible gambles in the search for oil. Modern wildcat wells cost from $100,000 to $2 million. One out of nine is a profitable venture. One out of a thousand is a bonanza. Yet it is the wildcatter who keeps the oil-and-gas discovery rate ahead of consumption. Once the discovery rate falls behind the rate of consumption, the colonel knows that oil prices are bound to soar and that national security, progress and prosperity will suffer accordingly. The depletion allowance also attracts billions of dollars in idle money. Not even the wildcatter and his normal financiers could buck the odds long without that money. The colonel has a clear conception of the depletion law (which its opponents call a tax loophole) and is its most eloquent defender. His statement to the House Ways and Means Committee (Appendix 1 to this book) is typical of his simple and effective method of stating facts. While the poorly informed, the demagogues, and those who compete with oil have and will continue to attack the law, the colonel's statement stopped one and will probably stop other such attempts.

In 1953 the Interstate and Foreign Commerce Committee of the U. S. House of Representatives also conducted an investigation into crude oil and gasoline price increases. The increases had been the first since the industry's prices had been pegged before the Korean war. Leaders of the industry, particularly some big company witnesses, had failed to impress the committee with their explanation of the reasons for the price hike. The committee, in turn, had been rough in its handling of the oil company executives. Independents had come off somewhat better. Thompson, who had no interest in and no authority regarding oil prices, was called by the committee to determine whether or not Railroad Commission oil allowable reductions had had anything to do with increasing oil and gasoline prices.

Contrary to the manner in which he had treated most of the big company oil executives, Chairman Charles A. Wolverton of New Jersey made an introductory speech praising the colonel.

"I have informed the committee that it would not be a real, full investigation or study of oil without the appearance of General Thompson," Chairman Wolverton said. He also recognized Texas' dominant position in the supply of oil and the influence of Ernest Thompson.

It took fifty-five legal-sized pages of single-spaced type to reproduce the colonel's testimony. He explained in detail how the Texas Railroad Commission operated, its history, the details and reasons for the market-demand law, and answered all questions on oil production or proration.

Throughout the testimony Ernest Thompson disclaimed any knowledge or interest in the price of oil. His interest was in conservation. But when he was asked if he believed the price increase was justified, he said he did. The available supply of oil had nothing to do with the increase, he pointed out. Costs had gone up constantly for materials and labor, oil was getting harder to find, wells had to be drilled deeper, with drilling costs rising geometrically instead of arithmetically as the bits went deeper.

The committee was assured that the Texas Railroad

Commission had never kept oil output low to keep prices high. He said the Commission usually permitted the production of more oil than the government's own Bureau of Mines had indicated was needed. Without good waste-prevention over the years, he said, that would not have been possible. Without conservation, including the market-demand law, he said, oil would either have been exhausted or would be in very short supply and prices would be many times higher.

The committee took no action against the price increases. Its respect for the integrity and knowledge of witness Thompson was complete. Even those committee-men who had sincerely believed the price increases were unjustified knew that conservation helped prolong low prices rather than contribute to higher prices.

It was 1953, also, that the Pentagon called on Ernest Thompson for a recommendation. It wanted to know what to do about the Point Barrow federal oil reserve in Alaska.

"Abandon it," the colonel replied. "It has no value, except to stand by for a possible emergency. You know what you have there and it isn't much. But if you do need it, you can always go back to it."

The off-the-cuff reply was not sufficient. The Secretary of the Navy asked Ernest Thompson to inspect the property personally and make a complete report. He agreed. Point Barrow was one of the wartime projects that had been developed at tremendous cost but had yielded little oil or gas. Thompson knew that about forty-five wells had been drilled there at a cost of about $47 million plus some $4 million annually for upkeep.

Dr. William E. Wrather, one of the nation's most eminent geologists and James S. Abercrombie, Robert H. Abercrombie, Wesley West, William A. Smith and Herman Brown, all of Houston, made up the Thompson party. All were practical oilmen. The inspection was complete, and the colonel's recommendation was the same as it had been in the first report.

Point Barrow was abandoned as a project and left in the hands of a small party of caretakers. Actually the field's total production amounted to only enough gas to keep its full housekeeping detachment in heat and fuel.

The twenty-two years that have elapsed since the colonel first came face-to-face with the unruly Black Giant from his field desk and canvas chair in the little pyramidal tent near Kilgore have been the most progressive years in the history of the oil industry.

Thompson, of course, hasn't done it all; thousands have contributed materially. They include all of his colleagues and many far-sighted oilmen, independents and major company men alike. But without his encouragement, drive and incisiveness the others might have accomplished little.

The colonel has drilled no wells; he has invented nothing. Many of the conservation ideas that have ultimately gone into effect were not of his own creation. His personal contribution reaches far deeper than any of these. If his most important contribution can be defined, it is perhaps the unswerving course he has charted and sailed and his ability to get others to follow it. By refusing to give way to pressure, threats, abuse or expediency he has frequently been the rallying point around which others of the same bent could co-ordinate their efforts. Some fights he has led. In others he has followed the leaders. But whether in the vanguard or the background, almost from Thompson's first hours on the Commission, the firm and steadying hand of the redhead from Amarillo has clearly been evident in virtually every progressive step the industry has made. When the going is toughest, he fights the hardest, undismayed by almost impossible odds or by the lack of support from his friends or even his colleagues. And because he is unshakable, he wins; sometimes quickly, sometimes only eventually. He has consistently been the hard core of determination that got the job done. In hundreds of courtroom battles Thompson and the Commission lost ten cases for every one in which they were victorious. It was the process of good law by trial and error. When the judgment favored the Commission, it almost invariably became a landmark case along the conservation trail. But it is typical of Thompson that every case lost served mainly to goad the colonel determinedly on to continue the fight until the best public interest was achieved.

When Ernest Thompson joined the Railroad Commission the oil industry had progressed from the lamp and lubrication days that started with Drake's discovery near Titusville in 1859. Spindletop had begun fueling the world in 1901, but the oil industry was still a shaky adventure for fortune hunters when Dad Joiner kicked the top off East Texas in 1930, the last of the big booms. It is significant that from the day Ernest Thompson took charge of things at Kilgore in 1932, the industry started to stabilize. Booms and boom towns vanished. In their place are neat, pleasant and efficient little oil towns with steady American families to oversee reservoirs that will last for many years instead of a few blustery months. From a wildcat promotion business for which no one could borrow a dime from a reputable financial institution, it has become an industry so secure and stable that banks in Chicago, New York, St. Louis, San Francisco, Boston and Philadelphia advertise for oil loans. In the oil country every local bank has a vice-president in charge of such business. The largest insurance companies eagerly make oil loans. Investors with idle money band together in syndicates to back oil deals based on scientific and technological reports.

In spite of lamentations in the late 20's and even since, when it was popular for some government know-nothing to predict that the nation was running out of oil, the industry has constantly added to its reserve capacity, even with market demand growing at the rate of 500,000 barrels daily each year. The producers, by employing waste prevention and good reservoir-control principles, are getting eighty percent of the oil out of an oil field instead of twenty percent, as they did before 1932.

East Texas, where the optimistic experts said a billion barrels of oil would be produced eventually, has already produced three billion barrels and probably will produce that much more. Thompson saved five billion barrels of oil! Few men in public life have been responsible for such a contribution to national wealth, energy and security.

Only a few years ago natural gas was a drug on the market; today it is the raw material for two of the greatest young industries in the world, petrochemicals and long-line natural gas, with Texas alone supplying twelve-billion cubic feet daily to make the nation more efficient and more comfortable. Again, Thompson is largely responsible; and this, too, is an achievement far greater than most national heroes can claim.

Time magazine, late in 1953, described Thompson as "a scholarly man in rimless glasses" who "presided over one of the most powerful regulatory bodies in the world . . ." and who has "dominated the Texas [Railroad] Commission as well as U. S. oil conservation practices. . . ."

The Associated Press recalled his announcement for re-election in 1948 when he used thirty-one words to dispose of the formalities and fifteen words to state his case: "I am thoroughly familiar with the work of the Railroad Commission and I enjoy it."

When Max Skelton, the AP man, reminded the colonel of that, his comment was simply, "That's about all there is to life—service and the enjoyment in being of service."

In other interviews he reiterated his belief that "the best place to store oil until you need it is in God's reservoir where He put it and where He kept it for millions of years until man was given the intelligence to find it."

He said he believed in a government of laws instead of a government of men. "Write it down so that no matter how bad the man is he can't get away from the letter of the law."

243

In a speech in Wichita Falls, Ernest Thompson said "There is nothing more important to mankind than the conservation of soil, water and oil, except the salvation of his own soul."

Oil men have a profound respect for the colonel founded on an admiration for his accomplishments. Many have fought his ideas only to lose and discover they were much better off for having lost to him. Some have a fear of him. They fear his frankness and his determination and the embarrassment he can dish out with a biting attack of logic.

The colonel's greatest rule of life is the rule of reason. He has a keen legal mind, and an amazing memory for names, facts, figures and incidents, He is completely consistent. He leans heavily on good friends and on technical, scientific and legal minds for guidance.

When Ernest Thompson went on the Texas Railroad Commission, there were twenty-three major oil companies and about 4000 independent operators. His critics said the conservation practices he advocated and the rules he enforced would drive the independents out of business. But twenty-two years later there were still only twenty-three major companies in the field, but the number of independents had more than doubled. That, plus the fact that oil had remained plentiful and its products have stayed cheap, is the fulfillment of his program.

No other one man in the history of public service of the United States has ever wielded greater influence over the economic welfare of the country. Ernest Thompson has done what he has done without fanfare and with simple dignity. His influence probably saved the nation's keystone industry from chaos and destruction. And he has done it without fear of criticism, favor to friend, or a bow to power.

He has accomplished what he has accomplished without investing a nickel in oil or taking a nickel out of it. All he has ever put into that great American industry is his life.

Appendix One

Statement
of
Lt. General Ernest O. Thompson
Chairman
The Texas Railroad Commission
Before
The Ways and Means Committee
United States House of Representatives, Washington, D. C.
August 14, 1953

Mr. Chairman and Members of the Committee:

I thank the Chairman for the invitation to appear today and discuss the oil and gas depletion allowance.

My name is Ernest O. Thompson. I am and have been a member of the Texas Railroad Commission continuously since June, 1932. It is an elective office.

Among the other duties of the Texas Railroad Commission, is that of conservation of oil and gas, administering our conservation statutes—waste prevention statutes.

I have no financial interest in oil. I own no oil properties, no oil production, no oil royalties, no oil stocks, no oil interest of any sort or kind whatsoever. So far as I know, none of my relatives owns any oil interest. My sole interest in oil is that of a citizen-soldier, and that of a conservation official.

In addition to being a member of the Texas Railroad Commission, I have long been a member of the Texas National Guard. I served in the first war as commander of a machine-gun battalion in the 90th Division. I remained in the Guard all the time between the two wars and trained two regiments in World War II. President Roosevelt sent me as his representative to the World Petroleum Congress in Paris in 1937. Secretary of War Robert Patterson sent me on a survey of oil and gas supplies throughout the European Theatre in March, 1945 and then to make a survey of the oil fields in the Middle East, which I did.

In 1951, I was one of the representatives of this government at the World Petroleum Congress at the Hague.

My interest has always been that of a citizen-soldier. For several years, I have been the commanding general of the Texas National Guard, so my thinking, naturally, is that of national defense. It is in this way that I have always approached the conservation of oil and gas. In the final analysis, oil is truly a munition of war.

It might be of great significance to point out to this Committee that the United States percentage of world oil reserves is constantly decreasing even with the present depletion rate. We now have twenty-three percent of the world's reserves; whereas, we produce over fifty percent of the world's oil production.

Moreover, we consume about sixty percent of the world's oil production.

It is my view that our consumption of oil and its products will increase as the years go by; and it is, of course, a fact that every oil field depleted means just that much less oil in our reserves. Oil is not replaceable. Only nature can make it so far as we know now. So we must encourage discovery and be good stewards when we find it.

WHAT IS DEPLETION ALLOWANCE?

Depletion is a recognition that every time you take out a hundred barrels of oil, there is just that much less oil in the reserve under the ground.

I think it might be well to distinguish between depreciation, which is an allowance to rebuild something that can be re-built, and depletion in oil, which is the recognition of a diminu-tion in the reservoir. Only nature can make oil. Man can only search for these deposits of nature.

DEFENSE NEEDS MORE RESERVE CAPACITY

Ten long years of strict conservation of oil and gas and prora-tion of production in Texas prior to Pearl Harbor, made it possible for our nation to have all of the oil it needed for the war effort in World War II. We were never short of oil, although I must say that we were severely taxed in our producing ability many times during the war. We produced our fields to the limit. We had no extra capacity to produce and rationing of civilian needs was necessary in order to conserve the oil.

Since World War II, I have kept constantly in touch with the oil requirements for our defense. For a number of years, I have been trying to ascertain from the Defense Department the answer to this question: How much reserve daily oil-producing capacity is enough for adequate national security? Here is the reply recently received by the Honorable Lyndon Johnson, our senior Texas Senator, from our very able Secre-tary of the Navy, the Honorable R. B. Anderson.

"This is further reference to your letter of 20 April 1953, concerning the question posed by General Thompson of the Texas Railroad Commission relative to the amount of reserve daily-producing capacity required for security. The Chief of Naval Operations, on the basis of investigation made in accordance with my instructions, has furnished me with information on your inquiry.

"The problem, as presented, is not peculiar to the Navy or any one segment of the government. It is closely related to problems of national and international scope and is tied in with the amount of oil reserves available to the Free Nations of the World.

"It is estimated that the current U. S. daily production, including crude oil, distillates, and gas liquids, is 7,059,000 barrels per day. The estimated daily production capacity if restrictions were removed is 8,159,000 barrels per day.

"This figure is not sufficient to meet the U. S. and Allied requirements in time of a national emergency. To meet the estimated wartime deficit, it will be necessary to resort to rationing as in World War II and a realignment of the petroleum end products as they come from the refineries.

"In addition, reliance must be placed on the drilling of new wells and development of areas heretofore not fully developed rather than putting all our faith in proven reserves such as Elk Hills and Teapot Dome.

"The problem is not one of reserves alone, but it is interrelated to refining capacity, land transportation facilities, tankers and storage facilities as well as increased drilling of wells and development of new fields.

"The Petroleum Administration for Defense under the Department of Interior is one of the agencies that coordinates the military requirements with similar civilian demands, and is in a position to elaborate on certain aspects of the problem that do not fall within the cognizance of the Armed Forces."

Signed "R. B. Anderson, Secretary of the Navy." Dated "22 May 1953."

This highly authoritative and carefully studied report makes it clear that we do not have enough oil for national security. This means that we must drill ever deeper and deeper and continue our search for oil until we bring in and build up at least another million barrels of reserve daily oil-producing ability. By reserve daily oil-producing ability, I mean the ability to produce the oil from already drilled wells.

The Secretary of the Navy points out very correctly that we cannot place our dependence upon undrilled lands set apart for so-called oil reserve. The only dependable defense reserve in oil is in wells already drilled and producing at rates below the maximum efficient rate so that come war, we need only to produce the wells at the full maximum efficient rate every day to bring forth the extra oil needed. That means extra producing capacity that you can count on just like money on deposit in a bank to your checking account. Surely this is no time to tamper with anything that might affect our national security. Rather, we should be hunting up ways to further stimulate domestic production.

We do not yet have enough ready reserve oil-producing capacity for our national security, not half enough. Revenue, however badly needed, cannot be considered when our national security is at stake. Our very freedom is involved. Come war, there would be no time to hunt for places to drill oil wells. That takes years at best. To be useful for defense, gentlemen of the committee, the oil wells must have already been drilled. Reserves lying undrilled are of no value and there would be no time to drill them; there would be no steel available for the drilling. The oil wells must have already been drilled, equipped and ready to produce, hooked up and connected to the pipelines and to the refineries of ample capacity, ready to make the products required in sufficient quantities and of proper quality.

Since the close of World War II, the oil industry has gone faithfully forward with new drilling, new pipeline construction, new refineries to the amount of more than $17 billion. They have done that in order to keep up with the ever-expanding American economy and to help get ready for the National defense in time of possible emergency. I feel that we should not now imperil the progress in this field and become dependent on foreign oil. Even in time of peace foreign oil may be denied us by political complications——witness Iran today. Such could happen anywhere. It did happen in Mexico in expropriation.

Make no mistake about it, gentlemen of the committee, a ready domestic oil supply will continue in the mind of our enemy to be one of the greatest deterrents of war. Oil is ammunition. In defense or attack, oil is a prime factor. It is my honest opinion that any reduction in the depletion allowance would be poor economy indeed. Why tamper with a system which brought forth a drilling program—which is the only way to find oil—and has made oil available in such quantities that we have been able to win two wars within a generation.

Men venture in risky drilling, largely because of the twenty-seven and one-half percent depletion allowance. Remove that incentive, and our domestic supply of oil will shrivel; and we will become, in my opinion, dependent upon foreign oil within a very short time. Come war, foreign oil, of course, could be denied us. Especially, is this true of the great Persian Gulf area, the Middle East, Iraq, Iran, Saudi Arabia, Kuwait and Bahrein Islands where they have discovered more than sixty-four billion barrels of oil. The production in that area has already gone up to 2,524,000 barrels of oil per day.

These great Middle East fields, gentlemen, lie under the very shadow of the Russian bear, right at the border. I have heard it testified in the committees of the Congress by high military officers that these oil fields could not be counted upon by us if war should come. Therefore, I urge the members of this committee not to change the twenty-seven and one-half percent depletion nor reduce it in any way. The system is working; it is producing the oil. It means national security.

We cannot afford to let anything happen that would lessen the incentive to hunt for oil in the United States.

EXPANDING PEACETIME ECONOMY NEEDS MORE RESERVE CAPACITY

We need additional reserve producing capacity for our ever expanding economy.

Each year our crude requirements are increased by 500,000 barrels of oil per day. It can, therefore, be safely predicted that by 1975, we shall need from twelve to fourteen million barrels of crude per day in the United States.

Gasoline consumption is up eight and three-tenths percent over last year. Factory sales of new motor vehicles in the United States last year amounted to 5,208,981, or an average of 14,232 each day of the year. The railroads have largely converted to diesels, which require much oil.

We have in storage at this time above ground 143,446,000 barrels of gasoline; but when divided by the number of vehicles on the road using gasoline—that is, automobiles, trucks and buses—that gives only 114 gallons per vehicle in storage today. This does not include farm tractors or stationary equipment.

NEW DISCOVERIES NEEDED

Consuming as we now do about seven million barrels of oil per day in the United States, it must be remembered that a million-barrel discovery would supply the United States for a little less than four hours. The discovery of a good field, say about a hundred-million-barrel field, which is a major discovery, would only supply the United States fourteen days. Only one out of 991 discoveries is a hundred-million barrel field. During the past ten years, there have been only nineteen such discoveries in the United States. Or differently stated, within the past ten years, we have discovered only nineteen oil fields each of sufficient reserves to supply the United States for fourteen days. Only four of these fields were of a depth of 5000 feet or less. The depth of the others range from 5000 feet down to as deep as 13,100 feet.

HOW CAN TWENTY-BARREL WELLS COMPETE
WITH 10,000-BARREL WELLS?

The average oil production in Texas today is a little less than twenty barrels per well per day. The average for the United States is around fourteen barrels per well per day. Some wells in foreign fields produce up to 10,000 barrels of oil per well per day. Our problem here in America is to find ways and means to permit our oil to compete in the world market with foreign oil. Our exports have been dropping. Imports of crude oil and products for the four-week period ending July 25, amounted to approximately 866,200 barrels daily.

This brings about, naturally, a question which faces the American people today, and that question is, "How can twenty-barrel wells compete with 10,000-barrel wells?"

Certainly, without the depletion allowance, the domestic oil producer could not stay in business and compete in the world market with foreign oil.

The average daily production of oil in Texas during the month of July, 1953, was 2,805,600 barrels per day. We had 142,650 producing wells on July 31st. If you divide 142,650 (the number of wells) into 2,805,600 barrels (the average daily production), you get approximately 19.7 barrels per day as the daily average per well production. Multiply 19.7 by $2.86, the average price per barrel of oil, and you get $56.34 as the average total gross revenue from each oil well in Texas in July, 1953. From this $56.34, there is deducted the one-eighth landowner's royalty or $7.04, leaving the operator $49.30.

Take from this $49.30 the interest on investment, taxes,

(and they are many) maintenance, repairs, labor, wages and other overhead expenses, and you will readily see what the producers of this country face.

Certainly it is fair to assume that if the depletion allowance is reduced, our supply will suffer. Many wells would be abandoned. Many new wells would not be drilled. We are not now in any position to see our oil supply diminished.

OIL HARD TO FIND

The search for oil is a hard one. New-discovery or so-called wildcat wells are successful in only one out of nine holes. Eight of nine efforts are failures, dry holes.

The chances of finding even a very small oil field are one-in-sixteen tries. By a very small field, I mean one that would supply the United States with oil for only four hours.

The chances of finding a small field are one in fifty-three tries. Such a field would supply the United States for two days.

As I stated before, the chances of hitting a major oil field are one in nine hundred and ninety-one. During 1952, the total number of exploratory wells drilled was 12,525, of which 10,090 or 81.2 percent were dry holes. Six thousand six hundred and ninety-eight new field wildcats were drilled, of which 88.9 percent were dry holes. In 1952, for every new field discovery, it was necessary to drill 43,862 feet of hole. This, of course, because you had so many dry holes.

The average cost of a wildcat well in the United States, including all exploratory developments and necessary overhead, is approximately $100,000. Many of them cost $500,000 up to $1 million and then prove to be dry. I know of one well which was drilled at a cost of $1,500,000 and which was dry.

Of all the wells drilled in 1952, 39.9 percent were dry holes.

Of all exploratory wells in 1952, 81.2 percent were dry holes.

I recently saw an analysis of the cost of finding and developing oil per net barrel of oil produced which was based upon the operations of thirty representative oil companies. This cost increased from $.55 per barrel in the year 1942, progressively to $1.57 per barrel in the year 1952.

CONGRESS DEPLETION-POLICY WISE

Twenty-seven years ago, in 1926, the Congress of the United States, after some troubles with discovery depletion provision of 1918, enacted the percentage-depletion law as applied to oil and gas for three purposes: First, to assure continuing abundant supplies for an expanding economy; second, to assure equitable taxation of the petroelum industry; third, to provide adequate oil reserves for defense.

This wise depletion recognition on the part of Congress has accomplished all those purposes.

Given a continuance of the opportunity which this time-tested method has provided, in my opinion, the industry will continue to find the oil as needed. It will meet the plea of the Government for additional oil-producing capacity for defense.

As further proof of the wisdom of the twenty-seven and one-half percent depletion recognition, I should like to point out that in 1926 the oil reserves of the United States in known fields were some eight billion barrels. Now, twenty-seven years later, in 1953, the reserves of the United States in known fields are approximately twenty-eight billion barrels of crude alone, plus about five billion more if you include natural gasoline, condensates and liquefied petroleum gases.

During this period of twenty-seven years, there were produced in the United States thirty-six-and-three-quarter billion barrels of crude oil. Now consider that carefully. Twenty-seven years ago when the depletion recognition was established by the Congress, we had in the United States only eight billion barrels of proved reserves. Since that time we have produced thirty-six-and-three-quarter billion barrels to meet current demand, and now find ourselves with proved reserves of twenty-eight billion barrels in the ground in known fields. I do not believe that stronger proof could be made as to the wisdom of the twenty-seven and one-half percent depletion. It works. It furnishes the proper incentive. It is dependable. It should not be tampered with.

GASOLINE CHEAPER AND BETTER

I have many times said that after all, it is the consumer who must be served. Served he will be. The consumer's interest will best be served by a retention of a twenty-seven and one-half percent depletion.

The average price of gasoline today in fifty cities, including tax, is 29.51 cents per gallon. Gasoline, like everything else, is cheaper and better where healthy, free competition prevails under a private capital ownership system.

With all of the increase in demand and with a tremendously improved product, gasoline today sells at a lower figure than it did in 1926, tax excluded. Two gallons of today's gasoline does the work of three gallons of 1926 gasoline.

We have built America by wise and efficient use of our resources. By wise laws we have given men the opportunity and incentive to find enough oil to make our great progress possible. Let us keep these wise laws unchanged!

Just last week our great President Eisenhower said in his report to the nation that "The collective resolve of the free world can and will meet aggression in Asia—or anywhere in the world." I feel sure this statement from our leader brought hope to the oppressed and enslaved peoples of the earth. It must have thrilled the hearts of every liberty-loving American.

256

This statement from our President makes more compelling the retention of every aid and encouragement possible to discover and develop more and more petroleum to guarantee as far as possible our security at arms in carrying out this pledge of world security from aggression and oppression. Oil is truly a must in munitions of war.

One of the most important reasons why the United States is great among the countries of the world is that it has strong, stable industries, one of the greatest of which is the petroleum industry.

Oil and gas play a vital part in the daily living standards of every American.

Oil and gas constitute the principal source of energy.

Adequate sources of these fuels are indispensable for national security; for example, more than one-half of all military tonnage shipped in World War II was oil. Texas furnished eighty percent of this oil.

The Federal Government has asked the oil industry to increase potential oil production by one million barrels daily in order to provide for adequate defense of our country. It is, therefore, inconceivable that any attempt should be made to reduce the percentage depletion allowance, which is the one incentive that has contributed much toward the oil industry's sound, solvent position in the national economy.

Oil and gas are natural resources which have no real value until discovered, developed and produced, and the biggest part of the value of oil and gas accrues when it is found.

Oil and gas are wasting assets. It can only be replaced by finding new supplies, that is, new oil and gas reserves; and, the finding of these reserves calls for extensive exploration programs, costing billions of dollars. On the average, a wildcat well costs $100,000, but some cost over $500,000. Only one in nine such wells strike oil; therefore, on the average, the oilman must invest $900,000 before he discovers one producing oil well. The manufacturer does not build nine factories before he finds one that will produce goods for sale, thus, the manufacturer spends $100,000 and is ready for business, whereas, the oilman spends $900,000 before he gets any production.

The big odds against the discovery of producing oil wells discourages the risk of capital, yet, unless money is risked to drill wells and find oil and gas, the nation will not have the natural resources it needs in times of peace and war; so, as a means of encouraging the hazardous search for oil, Congress has provided the incentive of percentage depletion.

Percentage depletion is allowed in recognition of the value created by the discovery of oil and gas. In the case of oil and gas, the investment in the property is not an adequate measure of the capital created by the discovery, because when we refer to depletion of underground deposits of oil and gas, we speak of exhaustible natural resources that, by their very nature, are irreplaceable.

Percentage depletion is essential to a healthy and stable oil-and-gas industry. It is a simple and practicable method of determining depletion deductions in order that the return of capital will not be taxed as income.

During the years 1935 to 1949, the oil-and-gas-producing industry invested just about twenty-seven and one-half percent (exactly the percentage depletion allowance) of the proceeds it retained from the sales of oil and gas in the search for domestic additional oil reserves. Percentage depletion is helping increase the reserves of oil and gas in many ways. As an example, it makes possible the orderly application of proration laws, conservation projects like water flooding, gas injection, etc., which are all very expensive.

The depletion allowance works in the public interest. For instance, in a twenty-five year period during which the incentive of percentage depletion has been in operation, oil producers have:

1. Invested approximately twenty-five billion dollars in the search for oil.
2. Drilled about 640,000 wells.
3. Discovered and developed forty-eight billion barrels of new oil reserves, more than one and a half times the volume consumed in that period.
4. Supplied six-sevenths of all the oil used in World War II by the United States and her allies.
5. Ended the twenty-five-year period with the largest proved reserves of petroleum in the history of the United States.
6. Developed the oil and gas resources of the United States to the point that they contribute almost half of the total mineral wealth of the nation.
7. Created an industry which today employs directly 1,500,-000, and indirectly many more thousands, thereby generating billions of national income subject to taxation.

The foregoing record has made it possible to produce more with less work; has made low cost transportation available to everyone; and has raised our standard of living. Because of adequate underground oil-reserves prices have been low, as evidenced by the fact that during the period from 1926 to 1949 wholesale commodity prices generally increased fifty-five percent, while at service stations the price of a better grade of gasoline, excluding gasoline tax, was almost a cent a gallon less in 1949 than in 1926, a decrease of three percent.

Some of the serious consequences from a reduction in the percentage depletion allowance are these:

1. The price of gasoline and other petroleum products will increase through added costs and scarcity.
2. The incentive for risking capital in the hazardous business of exploring, wildcatting, discovering and developing oil-and-gas reserves will be dangerously diminished.
3. The diminishing of discovered underground oil reserves

will jeopardize America's program of defense and military preparedness.

4. The small "stripper well" operator will be forced to curtail operations. Indeed, many of them may be forced to liquidate.

5. Because of curtailed operations suppliers to the oil and gas industry will suffer; and thereby less income will be available for taxation to the government.

6. Reduction of the industry's payroll will materially reduce individual income subject to taxation.

7. The millions of industry stockholders will not only get smaller dividends, but their incentive to invest in oil stock will be destroyed, resulting in a further reduction of income available for taxation.

The present depletion allowance should be preserved. When our oil reserves are increased, we add to our national income and, therefore, increase our tax revenue. We also, thereby, strengthen our military defenses. By this I mean that reducing depletion percentage would actually not increase the government revenue. On the contrary, it would actually reduce incentive to hunt for oil and gas and would therefore bring in less revenue and weaken our national defense. Further, it would weaken our strength for our ever expanding economy.

I trust the twenty-seven and one-half percent depletion recognition will not be disturbed. It is a wise provision. It truly protects the consumer by an assured supply.

A CONSISTENT TAX POLICY REQUIRED

The large amount of capital risked in the search for oil is recovered over a long period of time. Many producing fields have a life of twenty to forty years or longer. Capital risked in the search for these fields has been invested on the basis that the principle of percentage depletion is thoroughly established and will be continued. This principle is not only a recognition of the unusual nature of the search for oil but also an incentive to the reinvestment of capital in order to assure supplies for the future. Under these circumstances, it is necessary that tax policy on depletion be continued and that uncertainty with respect to possible changes in percentage depletion be removed. The very threat of possible change in the tax provisions with respect to depletion can act to discourage the necessary investment of risk capital in the search for oil. We cannot afford to discourage the search for oil, since it is taking an increasing effort to supply us with the oil that we are using. With the continual increase in demand and the steadily rising costs in the search for oil, the incentives for risking capital in the search for oil need to be increased rather than to be reduced as would be the case if any reduction or restriction were made on the present provisions relating to depletion.

Appendix Two

AN INTERSTATE COMPACT TO CONSERVE OIL AND GAS

ARTICLE I

This agreement may become effective within any compacting state at any time as prescribed by that state, and shall become effective within those states ratifying it whenever any three of the States of Texas, Oklahoma, California, Kansas and New Mexico have ratified and Congress has given its consent. Any oil producing state may become a party hereto as hereinafter provided.

ARTICLE II

The purpose of this Compact is to conserve oil and gas by the prevention of physical waste thereof from any cause.

ARTICLE III

Each state bound hereby agrees that within a reasonable time it will enact laws, or if laws have been enacted, then it agrees to continue the same in force, to accomplish within reasonable limits the prevention of:

(a) The operation of any oil well with an inefficient gas-oil ratio.

(b) The drowning with water of any stratum capable of producing oil or gas, or both oil and gas in paying quantities.

(c) The avoidable escape into the open air or the wasteful burning of gas from a natural gas well.

262

(d) The creation of unnecessary fire hazards.

(e) The drilling, equipping, locating, spacing or operating of a well or wells so as to bring about physical waste of oil or gas or loss in the ultimate recovery thereof.

(f) The inefficient, excessive or improper use of the reservoir energy in producing any well.

The enumeration of the foregoing subjects shall not limit the scope of the authority of any state.

ARTICLE IV

Each state bound hereby agrees that it will, within a reasonable time, enact statutes, or if such statutes have been enacted, then it will continue the same in force, providing in effect that oil produced in violation of its valid oil and/or gas conservation statutes or any valid rule, order or regulation promulgated thereunder, shall be denied access to commerce; and providing for stringent penalties for the waste of either oil or gas.

ARTICLE V

It is not the purpose of this Compact to authorize the states joining herein to limit the production of oil or gas for the purpose of stabilizing or fixing the price thereof, or create or perpetuate monopoly, or to promote regimentation, but is limited to the purpose of conserving oil and gas and preventing the avoidable waste thereof within reasonable limitations.

ARTICLE VI

Each state joining herein shall appoint one representative to a commission hereby constituted and designated as the Interstate Oil Compact Commission, the duty of which said Commission shall be to make inquiry and ascertain from time to time such methods, practices, circumstances and conditions as may be disclosed for bringing about conservation and the prevention of physical waste of oil and gas, and at such intervals as said Commission deems beneficial it shall report its finding and recommendations to the several states for adoption or rejection.

The Commission shall have power to recommend the coordination of the exercise of the police powers of the several states within their several jurisdictions to promote the maximum ultimate recovery from the petroleum reserves of said states, and to recommend measures for the maximum ultimate recovery of oil and gas. Said Commission shall organize and adopt suitable rules and regulations for all conduct of its business.

No action shall be taken by the Commission except: (1) By the affirmative votes of the majority of the whole number of the compacting states, represented at any meeting, and (2) by a concurring vote of a majority in interest of the compacting states at said meeting, such interest to be determined as follows: Such vote of each state shall be in the decimal proportion fixed by the ratio of its daily average production during the preceding calendar half-year to the daily average production of the compacting states during said period.

ARTICLE VII

No state by joining herein shall become financially obligated to any other state, nor shall the breach of the terms hereof by any state subject such state to financial responsibility to the other states joining herein.

ARTICLE VIII

This Compact shall expire September 1, 1937. But any state joining herein may, upon sixty (60) days notice, withdraw herefrom.

The representatives of the signatory states have signed this agreement in a single original which shall be deposited in the archives of the Department of State of the United States, and a duly certified copy shall be forwarded to the Governor of each of the signatory states.

This Compact shall become effective when ratified and approved as provided in Article I. Any oil producing state may become a party hereto by affixing its signature to a counterpart to be similarly deposited, certified and ratified.

Done in the City of Dallas, Texas, this sixteenth day of February, 1935.

INDEX

INDEX

INDEX

INDEX

ABOUT THE AUTHOR

JAMES ANTHONY CLARK'S column, "Tales of the Oil Country," is a special feature of the *Houston Post*. Mr. Clark is the co-author of *Spindletop* and he is an oil writer and historian. He was a lieutenant colonel in military intelligence in World War II in the original occupation of Korea, where he was in charge of communications intelligence after serving in the combat zone in the Pacific during the war.

Mr. Clark was a former statehouse correspondent in Austin, Texas; a columnist and correspondent in Washington and oil editor of several leading Southwestern newspapers.

Born in Abita Springs, Louisiana, and reared in Beaumont, Texas, Mr. Clark has been a resident of Houston, Texas, for the past fifteen years. He has worked as a boilermaker's helper in an oil refinery, as a roustabout on drilling rigs in south Texas, and managed a natural-gas company for the fabulous Glenn McCarthy. He is an associate member of the Houston Geological Society, and an active member of the National Association of Petroleum Writers.

Mr. Clark was the director of publicity, public relations and advertising for the year before the opening and for the first year of Houston's Shamrock Hotel. When not writing, he is a public relations consultant, in partnership with John D. Kemp, the junior member of the James A. Clark Company, who also serves as chief researcher and adviser in the book-writing end of the same business.

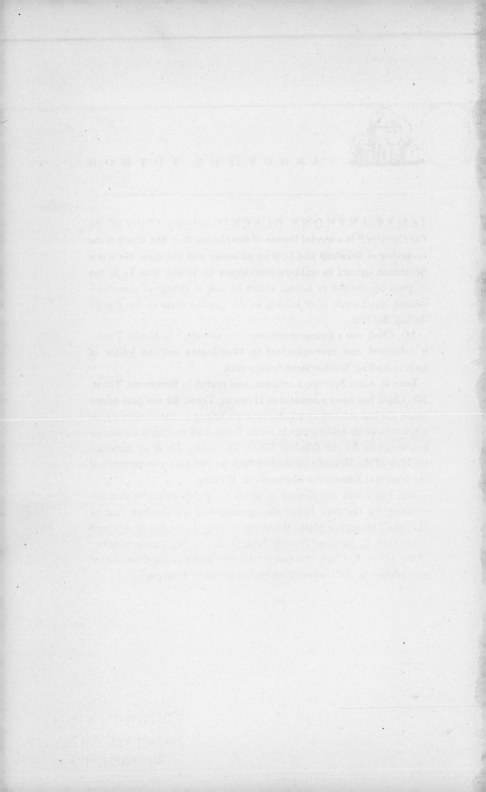